LARRY G. HARCUM

Laurie,
Hope you
enjoy

HLH Press
Virginia Beach, VA

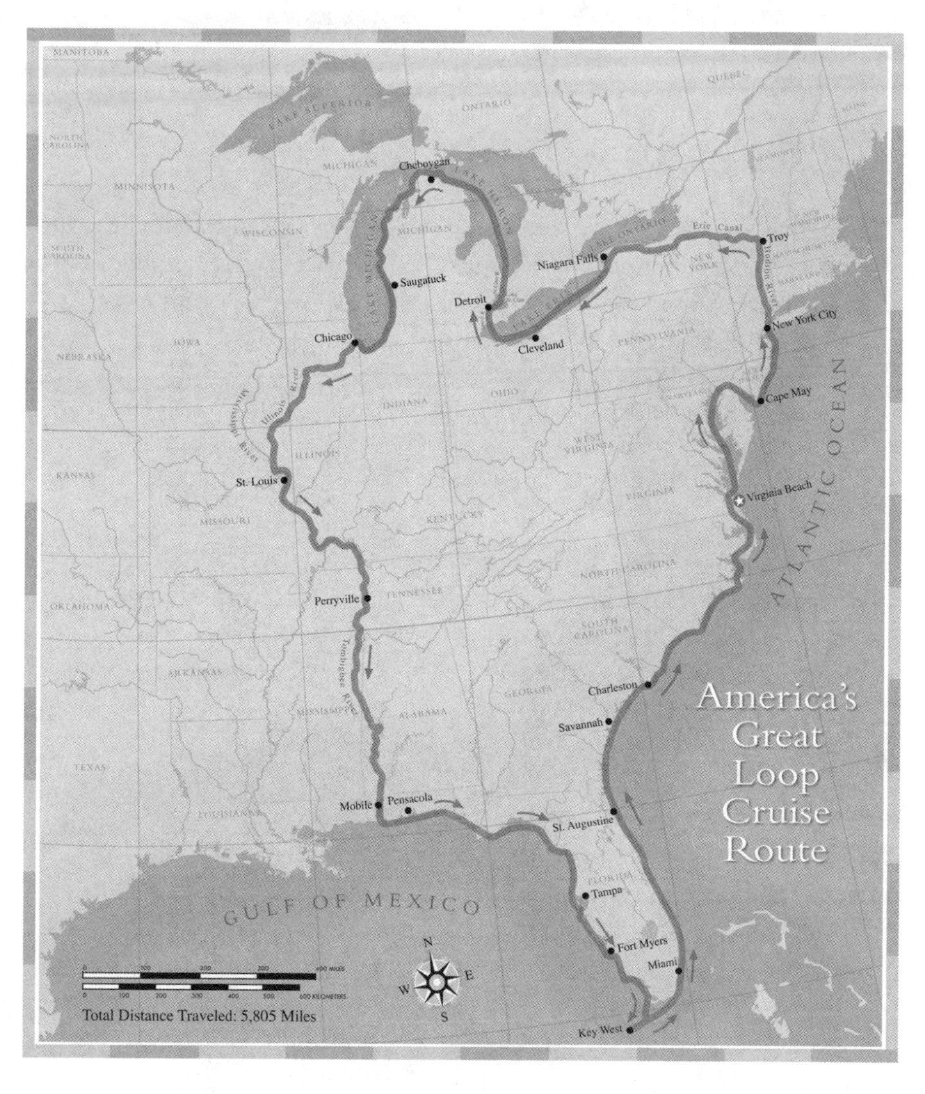

This map shows the route and some of the ports Larry Harcum visited as he traveled America's Great Loop.

Published by HLH Press
P.O. Box 801
Virginia Beach, VA 23451

Publisher's Cataloging-in-Publication Data
Harcum, Larry G.

DreamRider : adventures on America's Great Loop / Larry G. Harcum. – Virginia Beach, VA : HLH Press, 2006.

p. ; cm.
ISBN: 0-9787750-0-7
ISBN13: 978-0-9787750-0-1

1. Boats and boating—East (U.S.) 2. East (U.S.)—Description and travel. I. Title.

GV776.E27 H37 2006
797.1—dc22 2006932614

Project coordination by Jenkins Group, Inc • www.BookPublishing.com
Interior design by Debbie Sidman
Cover design by Chris Rhoads

Printed in the United States of America
11 10 09 08 07 • 5 4 3 2 1

Dedicated to my mom. A lady who loves me.

Contents

Disclaimer

I met a lot of people on this great adventure, but I have changed their names to protect them from my stupidity. The information about cities, places, and events is my best recollection but is in no way meant to harm this great country or any individual or group of people. Not all of the information is totally accurate; this book was written through my personal perception of events and people, with all those inherent inaccuracies. I tried to be as factual as possible, but to err is human. The events happened as described, but some are expanded or changed slightly for the sake of the narrative. Some of the individuals were composites or recalled as best I could. The material in this book is not meant as a recommendation or a denigration of any product, place, or person. I told the story as I remember it, with only small modifications for the sake of narrative, but I am not a camera or a tape recorder. All is recorded through my perception; perception can be flawed.

Preface

Take the dream and make it a reality. That's what this book is about—nothing more and nothing less. Just like you, I have pipe dreams and always want more out of life. Yes, we're all trying to grab a little slice of heaven. But if you want them badly enough, dreams can become a reality.

A famous person once said to write down what you want to accomplish in your life and make a top-10 list. Put this top-10 list away and look at it every five years and see how you are doing. You will be pleased or disappointed at your progress. If disappointed, possibly you never got your priorities right in the first place, so go back and rewrite your top-10 list. But keep in mind that each time you rewrite, you are five years further down the line.

I made a top-10 list when I was 23 years old. Much to my amazement, it never changed. Yes, there were setbacks and modifications along the way, but the basic BIG 10 never changed. To retire by age 50 was a goal. It was number 4 on my list. Number 5 on the list was "not to have to worry about money" when I retired. No, I did not need to be a millionaire; the key words there were: "Not to have to worry about money." I not only worked 9 to 5, but also I often worked 24/7. I did whatever it took to make my company successful. Add a lot of luck, right time, right place, right people, and bingo! I retired, or as I, with my Southern dialect call it, "retuired," at 50, or three days before I was 51.

Write down your goals and dreams. Check on them regularly. Then figure out specifically what your dream is. If you want to climb a mountain, what mountain, where, and when? How old can you be and still do it? If you want to paint a great picture, what kind of training does that involve? How do you get that training? How many hours of your day can you devote to this desire? Does it matter if the world counts it as great or only if you do? If you want to do it, begin.

There is a space between the dream and the reality. That's where most people get lost. Often it's just that we can't quite see what next step we should take toward our dream. There may come a point after you've done all you can (research, preparation) that you have to take the leap and just go for it. But you have to begin to fill that space between the dream and the reality to make the dream happen. There are small steps of reality toward the dream. How do you actually get from here to there?

The biggest space may just be the deep inability to believe that it (the dream) will really happen. So many things we live with today and take for granted would have been utterly impossible to previous generations. Even a few decades ago, the Internet would have seemed like something out of a sci-fi film. Walking on the moon, trips to Mars, skyscrapers—all would have been fantasy and subject to ridicule. Today, they are reality. Somewhere, someone took the first step, possibly not always knowing where those following steps would lead.

Everybody has his or her individual dream. It may be to go Mars or to be able to run the 10 blocks down to the local store. Both dreams are equally important. In dreams, we find ourselves—in the pursuit. Often, these days, we're convinced that only enough money will allow a dream. If you don't have the money, see how much of your dream you can reach without it. You might be very surprised. If you don't believe your dream will ever be real, try making one little part of it real. If it's to run a mile, try running 10 feet or 5 feet. You'll be surprised at how willing the universe is to cooperate with the dreamer.

I fulfilled my top-10 list by the time I was 50. I retired with enough money not to worry. It took a lot of years of hard work. But as soon as I reached that dream, new dreams began to develop. The satisfaction that came from the realization of my young dream gave birth to a new dream. That is inevitable. Dreams make dreams.

My next dream was to do the Great American Loop. The Great American Loop is a water route "looping" the eastern part of the United States—from the Atlantic, across the Erie Canal, through the Great Lakes, down the Mississippi, and around the Gulf and Florida. Why did I want to do it? I'd spent most of my life on the Chesapeake Bay and had grown up on the water, but life on the water had remained a mostly local adventure. The minute I discovered the Loop, something in me wanted to do it. We may not always know why we want to do something. Do we have to know why? Something in the spirit wants to go there. I wanted to travel the water loop around the United States and truly experience it. I wanted to learn more about the country I was born in, about the landscape of this birthright, about the people who lived along all those waterways. I did.

Because I had fulfilled my dream of having enough money not to worry, I had the finances for the next level of the dream. But doing the Great American Loop took planning and lots of detail work. Doubtless, it will be the same with your dream. Get specific. What exactly in research, money, backing, and planning is required to complete your dream?

As the guy in the movie said, "If I a man doesn't have dreams, he has nightmares."

Dreams change with time and circumstances. The dream you had at 20 may not be the dream you have at 40 or 60. Accept those changes. Allow that changes happen to all of us and go with those changes. As your awareness of self and others changes with time so, often, will your dreams. Or if you have an old, old dream you've never lost, there is a reason that dream stays with you. Don't ignore it—be it a new dream or an old. It is a part of your soul that is asking permission to live. All you have to do is grant that permission.

That is not to say you won't meet obstacles or that by saying yes to your dream it will instantly appear. Yes, the obstacles are real. You will have to pay a price for your dream. Most aren't willing to do so. Most people expect life to give them what they want. That isn't what happens. If you want to fulfill your dream, you are the one in control. It is up to you to make the dream happen. You can't sit by and wonder how it happens or why it didn't happen to you. You must make it happen.

Don't let the obstacles get more real than the dream. There will be daily obstacles—often they're simply trying or annoying. Sometimes they are big and apparently overwhelming. The dream killer comes in all sorts of manifestations. It is usually that one big "but." "But I don't have the money." "But I don't have the time." "But I'm not strong enough, lucky enough, rich enough, blessed enough." There's an endless list of "buts." We all know them. We've all heard them. We've all said them to ourselves. "But" is the dream killer. Just stop listening to it. Listen to the part of you that says you can do it and start to figure out exactly how. Walk into that space between the dream and the reality.

A dream is a vision, a hope, a projection of self into the future. You need to connect that vision to the realities you live in. Learn how to build the concrete bridge from here to there. It can be done. People do it every day. So can you.

This book is about how I completed one of my dreams. It took planning and research and hard work. It took the willingness to plunge into it. I had regrets along the way and frustrations and worries. Nothing goes completely as planned. If it did, it wouldn't be life but a movie script. Accept that things will happen on the way to your dream that you can't anticipate. And when your dream happens, enjoy it. Grab hold of that moment and take it in.

My dream was to do the Great American Loop. Along the way, I found more than my dream. I found an America I didn't know existed. I met people I would never have met. I discovered and experienced a landscape not before known to me. The world opened up for me. The dream always involves more than the immediate object. It involves a journey of the spirit, and along that journey, no one can say what he or she will discover—that's the joy and mystery of it.

In traveling the United States, I learned so much about this country that I hadn't known before. You can truly know by experiencing. I also

Follow the dream

learned a lot about myself that I hadn't known. The journey outward is often the journey inward. Those two worlds are not so separate.

I hope this story of my adventure will help you reach for your dream, whatever it is. This is a real adventure, not something Hollywood dreamed up. If Hollywood wrote this, it would be a much different story. But it is a dream that became reality, and reality is where the blood moves, the heart thumps, and the spirit soars. Move that dream into reality and you'll feel it pulsing.

America is the land of dreams. Because of that, this country has left its mark on history and civilization. If we forget those dreams, there will be nothing special about us anymore. If we get mired down in trivia and the daily routine that can often be deadening, we lose ourselves. America was made one dream at a time.

Set your spirit free. Live your dream. It can be done.

Chapter 1
Impossible Dream

There it was. I glanced at that picture I tore from a magazine and posted on my bulletin board at least 10 times a day. It was a painting of a little canoe floating along on the Tahitian waters, with a lovely brown-skinned girl paddling toward heaven. I could smell the water and feel the sun and the soft breeze.

The phone rang. I picked it up for the thirtieth time that day and answered the questions of another concerned depositor.

As I talked, my eyes went back to the canoe and the water and that beautiful woman just waiting for me out there on the water. She was going to be gray-haired by the time I got there.

"Bet it never happens," Jim said with a wink. Jim was a middle-aged coworker who never tired of teasing me about my daydream.

I winked back and then tapped the map on my bulletin board. It was a map of the eastern United States with the route of the Great American Loop outlined in ink. The Loop was a water route that circled the eastern United States up the Atlantic, through the Erie Canal and the Great Lakes, down the Mississippi, and back out in the Gulf, ending at the starting point on the East Coast, Virginia Beach.

"Want to take odds I can do this?" I asked.

"Sure, buddy, sure," Jim said with a cynical, knowing voice.

I was just about to press Jim into some real numbers and cash when Tom Wilkins came in with that look in his eye.

"Ms. Boeing?" I asked.

Tom nodded.

"Did you fire her up?"

"You do it," Tom said. He'd just dug it out of the mess of someone pushing the wrong button, and he didn't want to be the one to be blamed if it messed up again.

"Ms. Boeing awaits," Jim kidded as I went by his desk. "Ten to one," he shouted behind me as I walked to Ms. Boeing's chamber.

"You're on!" I shouted back. "Now! Cash. I will do the Great American Loop."

Jim pulled out a ten and said, "But it has to be within the year."

"Within the year?" I hesitated and then proceeded on my walk to Ms. Boeing while Tom walked nervously beside me.

"What's the Great American Loop?" Tom asked.

"Tell you later," I muttered. I hadn't taken Jim's bet. The Loop in one year was impossible. Jim always had to remind me of my failed daydream, particularly when Ms. Boeing was acting up.

I was in the bank's operations center. From there, we kept all the branches of the bank up and running. We made sure all the balances and deposits and withdrawals were current, accurate, and posted for the day, along with the electronic information throughout the bank. There were about 40 employees in the building. I was the operations officer and jack-of-all-trades manager, which meant I was in charge of making sure the nuts and bolts worked. It was an around-the-clock job and had been particularly intense the past few years—so intense I'd sold my boat. I just didn't have the time to get out on it anymore.

I had been doing it for almost 25 years. That day was Tuesday. I hated Tuesday because that was the day when all the checks written from the weekend hit the operations center. And, of course, today was the day Ms. Boeing was acting up again. As I walked through the 20,000-square-foot modern office building, the other workers looked up from their computers. If Ms. Boeing was having a real fit, soon they would be twiddling their thumbs too.

Ms. Boeing was a check-grabbing machine. It was a $200,000 machine, more than 15 feet long, with rollers and binds that processed about 1,200 checks a minute. It was the heart of the operation. Usually the problem with the machine was that someone had pushed the wrong button. Nine out of 10 times, that was it. If someone had hit the wrong button and uploaded new information onto the old program, then we had a jumbled mess. I'd have to reload the backup information from the previous day. It was 2 p.m. We'd have to reload and get current for the day and still get everything posted and up by 8:00 the next morning. The phones were ringing incessantly. The problem was filtering down. People got rowdy when they couldn't get their bank balance information.

Ms. Boeing was in a self-enclosed room with special noise-reduction pads on the walls. With a lot of metal and moving parts, it literally grabbed each document and ran it through like a conveyer belt, separating the items and putting all the deposits in one bucket, all the withdrawals in another, and all the checks for the Federal Reserve in another. Information was coming in from 10 locations.

We'd named it Ms. Boeing because when you fired her up, the noise was like a 747 jet taking off. Time to test the machine. The trays of checks and deposits were ready. "Let her rip," I said and started it. She took off with the usual roar, and then she crashed. Ms. Boeing slammed to a halt with a bang that would bring back the dead. The noise was shattering. The alarms rang. Checks and deposit tickets slammed down the runway and came to a halt. There were at least 300 items mutilated, spindled, and mangled. It was ugly. Ms. Boeing was having a bad, bad day. I hated Tuesdays.

I spotted three coworkers and signaled, "You, you, you! Come on. We got to figure this out. Let's find out what's gone wrong."

Four of us set to work to solve the problem. The check grabber was expensive to make and expensive to operate. It was as critical as any computer system. Like airplanes, they didn't make many of them. Information was stacked in a tray by it: deposit tickets, checks, loan payments, all kinds of transactions, and the machine had to read all of it. Reading 1,200 pieces of paper a minute, Ms. Boeing created the computer file that was at the core of operations.

"Let's open it up," I said. It had to be opened and maintained and cleaned regularly. None of us saw the immediate problem.

I could hear the phones blasting in the background. I'd been there before. It would only get worse as long as Ms. Boeing was down.

I glanced at my watch; it was 2:30 in the afternoon. That machine had to be up and running in time to post all the deposits and withdrawals by 8 a.m. the next day. I got the technician on the line. I explained the symptoms, and just like a doctor, he looked it up in his manual. "If it does this, go to x, and then if not, return to z ...," and so forth. By this process of elimination, we narrowed down the possible problem.

Electro/mechanical equipment was temperamental. Mixing electronic computer boards and hard metal moving parts could create a nightmare. I had lived with Ms. Boeing for 15 years, and I knew a lot of her likes and dislikes. I always questioned the technician and double-checked that the main headquarters agreed with the medicine prescribed. The technician was in Richmond, and it would take him two hours to get to Virginia Beach. He thought it was the sensors. The minute I hung up, I called him back again. "Bring two of those," I said.

If one failed, we had to have the other right away. Then I called the airport. The headquarters for Ms. Boeing's manufacturer were in Durham. The last plane from Durham came in at 9:00, allowing 45 minutes for the ride to the operations center—near 10 p.m. If we had to bring in something from Durham, I wouldn't know for sure until the technician from Richmond worked on it. He was still two hours away.

Jim walked by in the middle of this dilemma and said, "I'm changing the odds. Make it 20 to one. You and Ms. Boeing are in it for life."

"Jim, I'd appreciate it if you got your report finished today."

Tuesdays sucked.

Just then, the new temporary stuck her head into Ms. Boeing's room and said, "The president of the bank wants you to call her."

"All right," I replied.

The temp looked shocked that I wasn't reaching for the phone.

"Thank you," I said. The temp didn't know that the president of the bank was my wife. Hell, most of the employees didn't know. It wasn't exactly in the employees' manual. It wasn't that I didn't jump from a lack of respect, but I was in the middle of another crisis.

All the workers looked tense and stared at me, looking for answers. I gave them my most reassuring smile. A lot of people needed Ms. Boeing to work that night and for their information to be posted in the records by the next morning. The light bounced off the cars in the parking lot surrounding the building.

The phone rang again, and I answered, expecting to hear my wife's voice.

"The bank's been robbed!" It was a branch manager.

Jesus. It would happen then.

"Anybody hurt?"

"No, I'm not even sure he had a gun."

"You did the right thing." I started down my routine. "Close the doors. If it's on the news, don't comment. Call the relatives of all the employees and tell them they're OK. Shut down all incoming internal and external phone calls to the branch." I figured I had the time to get over there and back by the time Ms. Boeing's technician arrived.

Tom Wilkins gave me a helpless and terrified look as I headed for the door.

"I'll be back in time for the technician!"

The bank wasn't robbed often, but it had happened before. Usually they didn't get more than a thousand dollars, but there was a procedure involved with the law and the employees, and I had to be there to at least get the procedure started. I figured I had just enough time to get back and deal with the check grabber problem.

As I went by my desk, I glanced at the picture of the Tahitian paradise. Jim's words echoed, "Bet you'll never do it."

I frowned and headed for the parking lot at a run.

The branch was about 20 minutes away. It was a hot, sultry July day in Virginia Beach. Traffic wasn't as overwhelming as it would be in a few hours.

I didn't hate my job. I liked my job. I spent most of my time planning so these sorts of emergencies never happened. It was an endless battle against future complications. When the worst did happen, like today, I had to be as ready as possible. I usually was. But it was still my goal to retire by the time I was 50. I had made that goal for myself when I was 23. I was then 50. What a stupid goal!

Somewhere not far away, the sun was drifting over the Chesapeake Bay water, and, oh, I wanted to be out there on the water right then. But my dream didn't end with a trip on the Chesapeake, which I had taken dozens of times in my life. My dream was to ride the Great American Loop. I wanted to travel the water route of about 6,000 miles that "looped" around the eastern half the United States. In my mind's eye, I could see the route I had memorized—from Virginia Beach, Virginia, up the Atlantic, past New York City, and then onto the Hudson River, through the Erie Canal (west), out into Lake Erie, into Lake Huron, around Michigan, and into Lake Michigan, following the Illinois River from Chicago into the Upper

Mississippi. Then I could go to the lower Mississippi River or the Tennessee River and Tombigbee River. Either route would drop me into the Gulf of Mexico. Then I would hang a left (east) and head for the Florida Panhandle and down the west coast of Florida until I hit Key West; then I would head back up the East Coast to Virginia Beach (a total loop), where I was sitting in heavy afternoon traffic.

By the way, I didn't plan to do the Loop in a boat, as you might imagine. I wanted to do the Loop on a jet ski. I was hooked—on the Loop and on the Bumblebee (my nickname for the jet ski). Yep, that was my dream. The Great Loop was a trip I had to do. It was just a question of how.

That was my dream. But this was my reality. Ms. Boeing on the blink, a bank robbery mess to clean up, and my wife wanted me to call, certainly on some bank business because she didn't make unnecessary requests. I glanced at my speedometer to keep the speed down. No point in getting a ticket to make the day worse.

I passed the boulevard that led toward the pier, which would take me onto Chesapeake Bay. There was no sign of the bay in all the traffic and lights and noise.

Most dreams grow slowly and usually have small beginnings. Mine was no exception. It wasn't surprising that my dream had something to do with water. I had been blessed to live on the Chesapeake Bay all my life. The water was a natural for me. The Chesapeake Bay had always been home. I worked the bay, fished it, surfed it, and played in it.

I had owned various boats, from a 12-foot runabout to a 42-foot yacht. Early on, I learned to respect the weather. First lesson: pay attention to the wind. Never underestimate 20-mile-an-hour northeast wind. Known as a "nor'easter," such wind could play havoc in the Chesapeake. Four- to six-foot waves coming over the bow (front of the boat) could be downright scary, especially if the boat was having problems. The waves didn't stop just because you couldn't cope or your boat was falling apart. I learned this never-to-be-forgotten lesson when running out of fuel on a 21-foot runabout. Running out of fuel was one thing, but getting caught in 35-mile-an-hour nor'easter was just plain stupid. We towed my boat in behind a friend's boat. I got on the other boat; my boat was following by a line. The wind kicked in over the Chesapeake Bay, and the water turned seriously choppy. Most boats were fiberglass, so I didn't think my boat would break up, but I did think it might take on water and tip and, after being submerged in salt water, it would be useless. The line snapped and tensed; my boat heaved and whipped. I seriously debated cutting my boat loose, even though it was the one thing I didn't owe debt on. After a long few hours, we finally got my boat in.

That mistake was never to be repeated. After that, all the boats that I owned and operated were always prepared with an "A" and a "B" backup plan. I never again attempted the water unless I knew that both the craft and I could handle the constant pounding of the waves. I never took the boat out unless I controlled it and had backups in place. I did not fear the weather, but I did respect it.

As was often the case with boaters, each new boat I bought was always a foot or two bigger than the one I had previously owned. I gained great experience with each upgrade but all at a price. Boating was a pleasure paid for with the high cost of boat maintenance. The saying went: "Your stupidest day is the day you purchase the boat, but your greatest day is when you find someone who wants the boat worse than you." I had no regrets about all the boats I owned, but upkeep cost money. Failure to do the necessary upkeep meant loss. Failure to maintain the boat was where most boaters lost their shirts. They got tired of putting money into the boat and never using it. Getting tired of the boat was OK, and not using it was OK, but failure to maintain your investment was not OK.

I sold my boat that year. The job rarely allowed me time to get on the water. At the age of 49, I was tired of boating and tired of the maintenance cost. Boating had become an expensive ho-hum, so when I sold the boat that time, I didn't buy another. I was out of boating and bored. I wasn't a golfer and had no other hobbies or sports. My daughter had left home, off to live her life. I was at a loss.

The traffic came to a stop, and I sat there tapping my fingers and went down the mental list of what I had to cover when I reached the robbed bank. An SUV pulled up beside me and was hauling a jet ski. When the light turned, I followed the jet ski down the street for several blocks until it turned off. I was dreaming just looking at that jet ski.

After I sold the boat the previous summer, a friend of mine asked whether I wanted to go jet skiing. I wasn't enthused. Jet skis from a boater's perspective were a pain. Running a 42-foot motor yacht and seeing five to six jet skis coming for your wake was scary. If you got jet skis on the bow (front) and the stern (back) of the boat, you just could not see where they were. What if the jet ski lost control or had engine failure or you lost control of the yacht? Yep, I had an attitude about jet skis. They were irritating.

But I was listless the day my friend asked me to go jet skiing with him. So off we went. It was a beautiful early summer day on the bay. The sun was inviting, and the water was also beckoning. I took the bars of the jet ski with reluctance, more to make my friend happy than because I thought it was going to be much fun. The jet ski took off. I whipped over the water at 30 to 40 miles per hour (slow speeds by today's standards). I engulfed the animal under the water. I rode it on water two feet deep, and I could land the jet ski on any beach. And I used muscles I wished I hadn't. And I could still keep moving all day for less than $20 in fuel. The experience was different from boating; it was immediate and rich and intoxicating. I was hooked! Yep—hook, line, and sinker.

Four weeks later, another friend and I were planning our first jet ski run on the Intercoastal Waterway (ICW). Ed, also known to me as Halflooper, was an old friend. The planned route was from Myrtle Beach, South Carolina, to Beaufort, South Carolina. It was about 186 miles, and we would have six days to make the round trip of 372 miles and get back to work. I had previously run several parts of the ICW with other boats at 10 to 15 knots, but I was not sure how this would work with a jet ski. Keeping to our plan, Ed and I took charts (maps for land lubbers), some clothes packed in plastic baggies, bathing suits, cell phones, extra engine oil, toiletries, line (rope), cash, credit cards, and an ATM card. Neither of us was an experienced marathon jet skier, but we both knew that at 40 miles per hour, we would get somewhere fast.

In late July, we started the trip. I dropped Ed at the boat ramp where our two rented Bumblebees were. (By then I called the jet ski "Bumblebee" because that's what it seemed like it was to me.) Ed's job was to tow my Bumblebee upriver about a quarter of a mile to the marina where the trailer and car were. I waited at the marina. And waited. No Ed and no jet skis. One hour later, Ed showed up at the marina and was towing my Bumblebee.

"Ed, where in the hell have you been?" I yelled as he pulled in. "This is a north- south waterway! How could you get lost?"

Ed started cursing. In a short time, I discovered why. Ed had tried to tow my Bumblebee with a line attached to the handlebars. You got it—one pull and he had tipped the Bumblebee completely upside down. (Hmm. Granted, this Bumblebee thing was new, but it wasn't rocket science to tow the animal from the bow hook.) The seat came off, the compartments opened, and all my stuff was floating downriver with the current. The Bumblebee had been completely submerged. Everything was wet. So I hated it. I tried not to show it, but I hated it. It wasn't a good beginning for my second Bumblebee adventure. On the other hand, I had cash to continue the trip, and all I needed was a dryer for my clothes, a cell phone (lost to the water), charts, and stuff—which I found at the first motel.

Aside from that incident, the trip was perfect. The air rushed over the top of the water. The light danced off the water, and the free spray lit up my spirits. The Bumblebee skipped the top of the waves like a surfboard. I was getting more and more hooked on the jet ski experience. The trip just cast the sinker deeper into my mouth.

Two weeks later, I purchased my first jet ski.

Right then, sitting in traffic, I wished I were on it. It would have been a great day out on the bay. Instead, I was pulling up to the small one-story branch office. Two police cars sat outside the building, with their lights blinking. I went inside and took control. I had done this before after bank robberies. I was really more worried about Ms. Boeing than the bank robbery since no one was hurt.

On my way back to the operations center, my mind went back to my jet ski adventures. Two weeks after buying the jet ski, the first week of September, I started my next jet ski run. The second trip was from Beaufort, South Carolina, to St. Augustine, Florida. The total round trip was 484 miles to be completed in seven days. By then, we had figured out what worked and what didn't. The weather was great, and the water was flat and glassy. We started in Beaufort, South Carolina. Our plan was to run three days south and return the same route. The run south was wonderful—palm trees, Spanish moss, and deserted sandy islands. It just could not have gotten any better—great motels and restaurants, at the marina by 4 p.m., just in time for happy hour. Yep, that was the life.

The return trip north was another story. In one day, we faced lightning, 35-mile-per-hour nor'easter winds, fog, and wet charts. We drank saltwater for three days and questioned our sanity repeatedly. I purchased a rain slicker on the second day to protect my skin from the sting of the rain (like needles). Ed wished he had done the same. By the end of that day, I wished I had purchased two rain slickers because all I had left of the one was the hood and part of the left arm. We both had learned a lesson, and in the future, we would listen to the weather report. And wear full wet suits.

But even facing Mother Nature and all she had dished out did not stop the desire for more runs on the Bumblebee. With each run, the learning curve improved. We had the Bumblebee marathon run down to a science, and our equipment just got better. The setbacks—on one trip, my thighs were so badly sunburned that I had to wrap them in gauze like a mummy—didn't dampen or lessen my desire to do another run.

The several runs during that first season with the Bumblebee just fueled my desire to push the envelope. I wanted to take the jet ski greater distances. But the fall was coming on, and my jet ski dreams would have to wait. So I started getting all the information I could on jet skis. That winter, I got my subscriptions to the jet ski magazines, searched the Internet for information, and talked with others about this new creature that I was enjoying. Even if I couldn't get out on the water, I was soaking up all the knowledge I could find about jet skiing.

Winter set in. It was cold, and summer seemed far away. One January day, I went to the West Marine, as I often did. Fate or kismet took me to the bookshelf, where I saw *Honey Let's Go Boating (The Great Loop)* by Rob and Eva Stob. What was the Great Loop? Being the inquisitive type, I bought the book. In one day, I read the book from cover to cover. Then I reread it five more times. There were several variations of the Loop, depending on individual choices. Overall, the trip could be from 5,300 to 6,000 miles, depending on the route. This one book triggered the need for more information. I was hooked! The Great Loop was a trip I had to do.

I told my wife, "I'm going to do the Great Loop."

"Sure," she smiled. She knew me; I was responsible and would never let anything disrupt my job or future funds. She figured it was a no-brainer to give me the accepting response. After all, she knew I would not do it.

It did not take me long to figure out I did not want a big boat again, so that left the Bumblebee.

"I'm going to do the Great Loop on a Bumblebee," I told my wife.

"Sure." She smiled that same smile again.

How would I do the Great Loop on a jet ski? That's where the trusty computer and the Internet provided the wealth of information that I would need to consider this adventure. On the information highway, I found out that a gentleman by the name of John Moffett had already circumnavigated the Great Loop. I was able to find only one news article about his adventure. He had traveled 5,601 miles, from Chicago to Chicago. I tried every trick in the book to find Mr. Moffett to no avail.

I didn't know John, but his picture on the Internet seemed to date him about 20 years younger than me. I looked at his picture, and then I looked in the mirror. I had to do the Loop. If nothing else, I had to do it for the geriatric set. No AARP for me!

When I got back to the operations center on that black Tuesday in July, it was anything but a trip out on the inviting water. The technician had just arrived, and I made sure I was back there with him as he began working. I tried to keep my mind on Ms. Boeing and all her possible problems.

If you wanted to make any dream happen, you had to plan. Just as I had planned all the shorter runs on the jet ski the previous summer, I would plan the Great Loop. Why couldn't I do it? The first things that came to mind were job and funds. Funds were, of course, always the big question. It was not just a question of the cost of the trip. There were also ongoing bills that had to be paid. I would have to have funds to sustain my lifestyle for at least 12 months. I went down the checklist of my assets. I did not want to use the cash reserve. Well, maybe I was lucky or just made lucky investments, but the funding was the easiest. After a little calculation, I knew I had the funds.

But there was still one major obstacle. Like every dream, I had a dream-killing "but" to consider. I looked around the office and at Ms. Boeing—that was it. The job. What was I to do about the job while I went off looping the eastern part of the United States? I worked for a very good company. But I doubted that anyone would consider giving me a four-month leave of absence while I rode a Bumblebee across America. With my wife, I was one of the owners of the bank, but I had responsibilities to fellow employees and the shareholders. And who would or could take my place at the job? No one. The company had more than 200 employees, and if one employee took a sabbatical, then how many would be waiting in the wings for next year? The odds of leaving the job were slim. And even if I did manage to get a sabbatical, I was taking a huge risk. Let's face it: if a company could get along without you for four or six months, someone might question whether you were needed at all.

So there I sat, fidgeting, wondering whether Ms. Boeing was going to fire up, and checking my watch every few seconds. If this repair failed, I had to have time to move into the next level.

But, again, my mind strayed. I had figured the Great Loop could be accomplished in four months. I could ask for a sabbatical knowing it would be refused and then advise the company that I planned to take the trip with or without approval. But how could I leave everybody in the lurch? Nobody wanted or could really handle my job but me. I was essential to keeping the bank operation going. Because I owned a lot of shares of the bank, I was the last person who wanted it to fail. It was my main asset.

Ms. Boeing was going to be up and running by midnight, and we'd have everything posted and online by 8 a.m. I was determined about that.

Just then, the phone rang, and it was my wife, a lovely woman if I do say so myself. She and I had run the bank for the past 10 years, since the original bank president (third partner) died. Her voice was professional, as I knew it would be. "I need you at my office in 30 minutes," she said.

"You do not know the nightmare I have here," I objected.

Not her problem; she was the president. She knew what I was like when Ms. Boeing was sick; it also meant I was sick. But I also knew she would not disrupt my job for something that did not have red flags all over it. What was it? Another exploding problem!

Knowing my status, I gave the old "Be right there." After all, she was the boss.

I mumbled to myself on the drive over, "Damn, this better be good, or I'm going to explode." But I also knew that she would not ask me to come to her office if it wasn't important any more than a monkey would walk backward down the road. I knew it was big.

Buyers had been scouting the bank. They wanted into the market. They could buy our 10 branches all at once or put in one branch at a time. A big bank would go for the buyout. Negotiations were stirring.

It all depended on how badly they wanted into the market and their private assessment of what the bank was worth. The last I'd heard made me think a buyout wasn't happening anytime soon.

Now other thoughts entered my mind such as "bad loan," a "real big bad loan," "internal fraud," "bank director had died."

Thirty minutes later, I stepped into her office with her.

"They've gone to $28 a share," she said.

"You're kidding."

"That's their offer, Larry."

"Advise the directors this is one that the shareholders would have to know," I said.

And that was when I knew. There was no way the shareholders were going to turn down $28 a share. We were going to be bought. That meant the operations center would be replaced with the new bank's operations center. After all, the new company had its own computer systems and computer employees. No need for duplication. That meant I was soon going to retire—and by the time I was 50, just as I had planned when I was 23.

I also knew my wife wouldn't retire. She wasn't ready, and they had a job for her. If she wanted to do it, she could take it—that was her choice.

But I had a date with a jet ski and the Great American Loop.

I allowed myself only a few seconds to smile because I still had to get Ms. Boeing up and going, and I had to do it fast. Most likely, it was going to be a long night.

Driving back to the operations center for the second time that afternoon, I found that my mood had completely shifted. My dream was going to happen. I knew it. I could feel the blood rushing back into my chest and arms. It was almost as though for an instant I was transported out onto the bay, riding free on the jet ski. In nine months, I wouldn't have a job. In nine months, I would be out of work. How lucky was that! The biggest obstacle to my dream of running the Great American Loop was vanishing. I was going to be free. But I still wasn't sure enough of the whole deal. Maybe the offer would fall through. A hundred things might get in the way of the deal.

In September it was official. The bank had been sold. And I had nine more months of steady, well-paid work while I planned the adventure.

After I discussed all the financial ramifications with my spouse, I mentioned the Great American Loop again, saying, "This is an adventure I want to do."

"Sure," she said, as I thought she would. But I was sharing the dream with her, letting her know it was real. Her response was the same as it had been, but the tone had changed slightly. She still thought I was kidding, but she wasn't quite as sure as she had been a few months before.

"And now, with the buyout, I can do it," I added, backing up my resolve.

"Yes, you can," she said. I could tell I had made some progress. She had decided that maybe I would do it, and if I did, she was willing to go along

Marquee at the start of America's Great Loop at Nick's in Virginia Beach, Virginia

with it. She was moving toward accepting my vision. I only had to keep reminding her of my dream. And I had nine more months to do that.

Knowing I would be released from work in April, I formulated a plan of attack. I put on paper exactly what I assumed I would need. None of the items was set in stone; daily research changed the list. But the following dates were certain:

Planning: October through February.

Launch date: May.

I was definitely out of dreamland and into reality. I knew it was going to happen if I wanted it. It was systems-go, and I would launch. One step for mankind and one leap to the Great Loop. Bye, Ms. Boeing!

As I came back into the office the day I knew the offer was $28 a share, I bumped into Jim. "Twenty to one? I'll take that bet."

"Larry, it'll never happen," Jim laughed.

Wanna bet?

Chapter 2
Leaving

It was launch day, May 24, I was at the pier at First Landing State Park, 64th Street, Virginia Beach, with the new jet ski in the water nearby. It was 7:30 a.m., and not even Ed (Halflooper) had arrived yet. Halflooper was joining me for the first few days of inaugural shakedown. I had to make another quick trip back to the house to get the water trailer for the jet ski. I also had another mission in my quick return home.

When I'd left the house, Betsy, my wife, had been asleep. I knew saying goodbye to her would be hard. She'd never believed I would really do the trip. I thought up until the time she went to bed the night before she didn't believe it. When I got back to the house, I woke her. She opened her eyes and looked at me, knowing in an instant that I was indeed going then. She was truly upset. I had seen

Betsy cry about three or four times in all the 24 years we'd been married. That morning she cried. I held her. Then she knew my mind was made up, and it would take a firestorm to stop me. Maybe it hit her all at once that morning because she'd refused to face it until then. She put her arms around me, and I kissed her. I knew I was truly loved. I also knew I didn't want her to come to the pier to say goodbye. I promised to call her each night. She was reassured knowing that, but we didn't discuss what would happen if I didn't call. I had prepared for every aspect of the trip, but I never went into that with Betsy. We both silently agreed it was better not to talk "worst-case scenarios."

I arrived back at First Landing State Park shortly afterward. It was only eight blocks from my home. It took only minutes from my house to reach Linkhorn Bay, which flowed out for about 10 miles into the Atlantic Ocean. It was a nice quiet day. The heat of late spring had arrived. I had been to First Landing State Park so many times over my lifetime, launching from there to take the waterways. But this was different. A part of me couldn't quite believe I was there, doing this. Right then. Finally. I was going to run the Great American Loop.

The Bumblebee and trailer are docked and ready to go

When I got back with the trailer, Halflooper had arrived, and so had a few others there to see us off. There were my mom and Halflooper's two teenager daughters, who would drive the cars back that had brought the jet skis. (Seems backward, two grown men riding jet skis while the two teenagers drive the cars.) D.K. Dalbon, a friend of 25 years, had made good on his promise to see me off.

The wind was coming out of the northeast at 15 to 20 miles per hour. Late May, early morning, blue skies with drifting bellows of clouds over the shimmering water. The grass by the dock rippled in the wind. It was a good day to start the trip. Only 6,000 miles to go.

"All set?" Ed asked, stepping down to his own jet ski.

Halflooper was going to go with me for a few days on the beginning of the trip. Ed was my age, about 50. He was a nice-looking guy, I guess, as far as guys went, but he did nothing for me. He was about 5'7", stocky build, and was tanned with shaved hair. I always thought he looked like a big cuddle bear. Ed always left me with laughter. When you put us together, there was no telling what would be said or done. (I guess to the average lady, we were foul mouthed, but to know us was to love us—or maybe not.) Ed was not overly agile, but he was not fearful when it came to the water. I had traveled with him on boats and jet ski trips. Through thick and thin, he was a trooper.

He was going to run with me on the water for a few days and work out any kinks that might develop. That was the shakedown part of the trip. Hopefully, any bugs would be worked out in the first part of the journey. But we'd already had many test runs for equipment, so I didn't expect that much trouble the first day.

"I hear there's a pool going against you," D.K. said.

"Are you serious?"

"Some guy named Jim. Twenty to one."

"I'll take some of that action," Mom said. Mom was past 80, 5'3", small and petite, a perfect grandma.

D.K. gave her the number to call, and Mom said, "I'm going to make some easy money on you, son. There's no doubt you'll finish this trip."

"Thanks, Mom." I hugged her. Mom was the only one who really believed I was going to complete my adventure. She was trying to hide her worry with the gesture. She'd been around water all her life; she knew what joys and terrors it held.

"What about you, D.K.?" I asked.

"Well," he grinned, "I won't bet against, and I won't bet for. But if you get to my motel in Fort Myers Beach, Florida, I'll take care of you."

"Meaning free?" I smiled.

"It's a lock. But first you got about 5,000 miles, friend."

"See you there," I smiled. In my life, I had traveled 6,000 miles by plane, New York to Los Angeles and back.

I was a Boy Scout at heart. "Be prepared" was not just a good motto; it was a necessity on this kind of venture. It had been a long nine months of preparation to get to that moment. I had double-checked my own itinerary. I had researched each purpose and piece of equipment for the journey. I had spent nine months preparing, absorbing any information I could find like a sponge, and checking my supports and backups. I felt as confident as I could be about my choices. Marine charts could save your life on this kind of a venture, and I had made sure the previous night that they were all onboard my small vessel for the first part of my journey. My Mom was going to hlep out and send me additional charts as I needed them because I didn't have space to store all of them for the whole trip. The cell phone and PDA had me wireless and in touch. Also included were a handheld VHF marine radio (for listening to Coast Guard and marine police and water patrol units); a waterproof AM/FM radio with a headset, small to fit into the tight compartment I'd designed for it; and a GPS unit, which I knew how to operate after much practice. The water trailer behind the jet ski held an assortment of necessary equipment, including a flare kit, flashlight, anchor, collapsible paddle, and two five-gallon plastic containers for

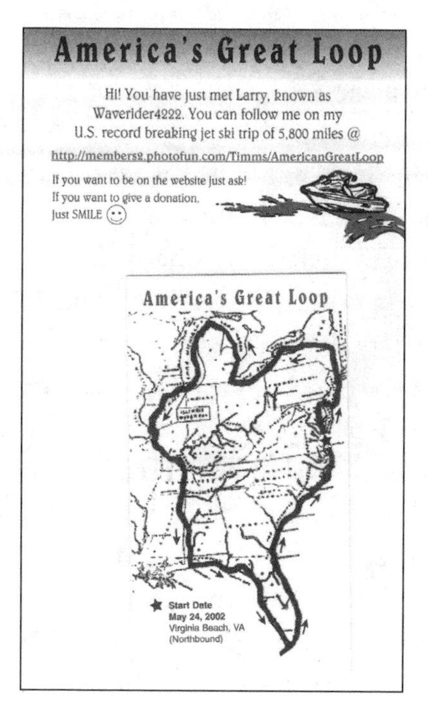

America's Great Loop
Hi! You have just met Larry, known as
Waverider4222. You can follow me on my
U.S. record breaking jet ski trip of 5,800 miles @
http://members2.photofun.com/Timms/AmericanGreatLoop
If you want to be on the website just ask!
If you want to give a donation,
Just SMILE
America's Great Loop
Start Date
May 24, 2002
Virginia Beach, VA
(Northbound)

This is a card I had made up to give to people on my trip

extra fuel, along with many other supplies. I even had business cards made up to explain who I was and why I was there (wherever I ended up) on a jet ski.

I stretched out my arms for a moment, trying to push off some of the tension. At 50, I was in good health and had no reason to doubt my physical abilities. But when I'd decided to do the trip nine months ago, I knew I had to be in better shape, so I began a regime of exercise. I'd spent the winter months walking on the treadmill and doing bench presses. That day I felt as fit as I would ever be for the beginning of the adventure.

While we exchanged pleasantries and Halflooper's two daughters, 17 and 18, looked around like "What's the big deal?" part of my mind raced ahead to the adventure. I knew what the beginning would be like; I had been on the Chesapeake Bay many times. But what about the Erie Canal, the Great Lakes, and the Mississippi? I wanted to see and experience it all.

I wanted to see a manatee. You might think that was an odd choice. Not exactly Moby Dick, was it? Having spent so much of my life on the water, I'd seen almost every kind of aquatic creation but that great gray elephant of the sea, the manatee. That thousand-pound sea creature loomed in my dreams at times, floating by with haunting grace. They could only live in the sea. They needed warm water for their slow metabolism, so I didn't think it too likely I would see one in the early part of the trip. Solitary, drifting the great seas, its huge gray mass gliding through the water, it was something I had often dreamed of. One might think I'd want to see a shark or a dolphin (I had seen and enjoyed both), but maybe it was only because I hadn't seen a manatee that it loomed large in my imagination. Seeing the creature had taken on a kind of symbolic importance, though I wasn't sure what it was a symbol for. With my attention on all the preparations for the trip, that old faint wish flickered across my mind again. I wanted to see a manatee.

And I wanted to meet John Moffett, the man who had already traveled the Great American Loop on a jet ski. I speculated that it might happen somewhere along the journey. Why not? I had already tried every way I could think of to contact him and had failed.

I had all the equipment I needed. The water trailer was hitched on the back of the jet ski. I had on my wet suit. The wet suit was made of neoprene (which did not deteriorate as quickly as rubber and was waterproof), had the thickness of a quarter, and normally was all black. It covered my entire body, with extra slip-ons for my head and feet. When you slipped it on, it stretched all over your body, and, in some places, it seemed to cut your blood circulation. The concept was simple: perspiration and water would be trapped between the wet suit and the skin, where it would warm with body heat. Keep in mind you were no photo model in one of these things, but it sure did work. But my first glitch popped up there: I had no wet suit gloves. I had standard gloves and thought the water would not be that cold that time of year. I would be wrong. I was headed north.

I climbed onto the jet ski, which was like a large bullet with handlebars. It was 12 feet long and weighed about 900 pounds and had a nice-looking gray and black fiberglass body. It was a new Yamaha four-stroke (the four-stroke had just come onto the market). With a deep V hull, the Yamaha was easier going over the waves. It was built to skim the top of the waves. I didn't call it Bullet. Instead I had nicknamed it Bumblebee; I called most jet skis Bumblebees because they covered the water like bumblebees—darting here and there, quick, held to no rules except of course the safety of others on the water.

That day, the Bumblebee looked great. I had appropriately added a few touches to make it my own. Linedudes (recoiled auto-retractable lines) were installed in a round plastic case mounted to the side of the Bumblebee. When docking for fuel, I'd pull the retractable lines out and attach them to a cleat. When finished, they recoiled back into the plastic container. No muss, no fuss.

A great car needed a great hood ornament, and so did a Bumblebee. It wasn't just any hood ornament. It was a full-wing American eagle. Damn, it looked good. With its great wings outstretched and its sharp features facing forward, it would lead me along my journey every day.

Then there were the passenger hand hooks, located on each side of the seat, used to secure the saddlebags with custom stainless-steel snaps to attach to the Bumblebee. The GPS was mounted so that I could clearly see it; it had to be able to withstand 60-mile-per-hour winds and four- to eight-foot waves. Then there was the flexible rubberized drink holder that moved with the Bumblebee to hold a drink in place. (And why not?) Decals. And the crowning glory, the American flag, fluttered off the back of the jet ski. I couldn't have been more proud.

I double-checked the water trailer hitch one last time. The trailer was just like the trailer behind a motorcycle but with no wheels. Storage on such a small craft was a major problem, and I went with the water trailer solution. It was about four feet long and weighed at least 200 pounds with all the extra equipment.

I'd had problems with the hitch during previous test runs. With the trailer empty, I had slung it around behind the jet ski and pulled it up and down with no backlash. Then I'd loaded it with 50 pounds and took off at 45 miles per hour and, pop, the hitch had sheared away from the Bumblebee. The heavy-duty plastic hitch wasn't going to hold. I contacted two local machine shops and had them work independently on the problem so I could get the best solution. One had replicated the hitch as hard steel, which weighed 20 pounds. The other company had covered the heavy-duty plastic with a steel coating, and that weighed five pounds. Assured by the salesman of the lighter version that it would be there when the pyramids fell, I bought it.

Halflooper was on a two-stroke jet ski that was reliable. After all, two-strokes had been on the water since 1972, so the engineering had been perfected. His unit was about 11 feet long, a burgundy three-seater. It made a lot of noise compared to mine. As usual, Halflooper had packed like he was going on a half-day picnic trip. On all the boating and jet ski trips we had taken together, he always had just one duffel bag. He could pack for a 10-day trip in 15 minutes. Halflooper figured that anything he needed he could get somewhere, even trying to borrow my toothbrush one time. NO!

We waved goodbye to everybody at the pier and pulled away. Seeing that my Mom was starting to cry, I turned my jet ski north away from the pier. We zoomed out onto the water. The water was calm, with winds blowing out of the northeast, about 15 to 20 miles per hour. The water temperature was 60 degrees, somewhat chilly and a good reason not to get wet. You could ride an 11-foot three-seat jet ski all day and never get wet.

Immediately I felt again the exhilaration of being on the jet ski. The wind hit directly in my face. The Bumblebee was darting eight inches off the water, and the water was as slick as glass. Speed, wind, salt water, smells, and out there nobody could catch me. Moving at 60 miles per hour, I was leaving a perfect wake. My lips were in a constant smile from the wind pressure. I knew there was no boat on the water faster than the Bumblebee. Unlike the motorcycle, I didn't have to worry about hitting another vehicle or vice versa. The waterways were open. Free. And you felt freedom on a jet ski. I loved it.

We were taking the route along the western shore of the Chesapeake Bay, that enormous waterway that cut into four states off the Atlantic. The mouth of the Chesapeake was about 20 miles across. Moving out to the middle of the mouth, we couldn't see land from either side. The bay kept closing up like the top of a pyramid as you moved north. At that point, it was just a lot of water with us following the compass bearing "north." The bay was mostly a north-south journey. The east coast of the bay was one long piece of land swinging down and out, with shallow water, marshland, and few places for safe anchorage or fueling stops. There wasn't much over there but mosquitoes.

The western coast, my route, was a series of jagged fingers of land where rivers emptied into the bay and large and small islands dotted the shoreline. The bay itself was not as moody as the Atlantic or as foreboding, but it had the ocean's saltwater. It was an enormous waterway that seemed to hold the rich memories of so much of the country's history, sometimes pleased and cheerful, sometimes dark and pleasing. Trees lined the shore; in the changing seasons, the leaves and colors reflected off the water in rich always-changing affirmations. The slope down to the water could be gentle and shallow or sharp and dramatic. Out on the water, about a mile from land, I reacquainted myself with this old friend, the Chesapeake Bay. I had known it most of my life, and, like any relationship, we were always in the midst of a negotiation, usually a wonderful exchange, even if the bay sometimes was a little on the rowdy side.

That day it was quickly turning rowdy again. It didn't take long to feel that 20-mile-per-hour wind on the water. Out on the ocean, the big waves were far apart, but on the Chesapeake Bay, the waves were close together. A six-foot wave was quickly followed by another, about three feet apart. I crested a six-foot wave, the water splashing over me, and another wave followed rapidly right behind. Each wave pounded the hull, and my speed slowed. I was down to 25 miles per hour. Each wave hit the jet ski and reverberated through my body. I faced the waves and maintained my balance. My grip on the handlebars tightened. There was a safety cord from my waist to the start button on the jet ski. If I got knocked off, that cord would immediately cut off the engine of the jet ski, which was preferable to having a thousand-pound jet ski loose in the water with six-foot-high waves hitting it. In those conditions, it wouldn't take long for the jet ski to tip over, and you'd have a nightmare on your hands. I glanced back down to the safety cord just as another wave hit the jet ski. All was well. If the worst happened and a wave knocked me off, I felt sure the jet ski would shut down.

I was only minutes out from the pier, heading west and north and away from the Atlantic. But already I knew things weren't going well for the home team. The problem was the water trailer that I was pulling behind the jet ski, loaded with my possessions for the trip. Each time the jet ski took a wave, the trailer followed it and me up and then back down with an ungraceful slam. Waves were close together on the bay.

But, as I said, I had gone through a lot with the hitch, and I was reasonably sure it would hold up to the beating. I was going 15 miles per hour. One wave after another. I would pull up; it would pull down. It would go up; I would go down. Again the jet ski went up into the air to take the wave. Pop. Behind me, the hitch popped off, and, in an instant, I shot into the express lane, jumping from 15 to 25 miles per hour. What a feeling! I slowed the jet ski and circled back. The hitch that was as durable as the pyramids had just broken into 10 pieces and was sinking into the deep, not to be found until the bay dried up and the pyramids fell.

I was only 25 miles into the trip and had just passed Mobjack Bay, a wide opening of about six miles with four rivers flowing into the bay. We weren't going to try for a marina with those rivers. It was too far to travel upriver looking for a marina with a limp trailer. The water was rough. I was going about five miles per hour, pulling the trailer with a rope. It was like pulling a wet mattress.

Meanwhile Halflooper was free to maneuver through the water with envious ease. I elected him to scout out any boats in the water and request the nearest marina. He found a fisherman who said the nearest marina was about 2 miles straight inland. So for the next hour we kept chugging west. In the future, all equipment guarantees involving the pyramids should be considered null and void.

The closest port was Gwynn Island, which was only appropriate, I thought, because my middle name was Gwen. The only choice was to lasso the trailer, tie it close to the Bumblebee, and chug to Gwynn Island. Moving at five miles per hour, a canoe could go faster than me.

Halflooper zoomed around back and forth. He did come close at one point and give me a reassuring smile. I wasn't sure whether it was playful mockery or reassurance. I wasn't sure either was in order. Knowing Halflooper, he was probably wondering why I had the trailer in the first place. I felt bad about it. I knew this wasn't the trip he'd hoped for. The game plan was to be traveling 150 miles up the bay at 35 to 45 miles per hour and into Solomon's Island before nightfall. I knew I was screwing up his holiday on the Chesapeake Bay. There was nothing worse than knowing you were making a friend's holiday miserable.

Gwynn Island was a triangle off the coast that came out into the bay. A narrow inner channel separated it from the mainland. Halflooper and I pulled up to a marina on the inside about a mile inland from the sandbar and the Chesapeake Bay. You would never know that four- to six-foot waves were pounding out there. I refueled the jet skis while Halflooper called home and got his oldest daughter to drive to my house, find the solid 20-pound metal hitch, and bring it to us. We were about 50 land miles away from the starting point. Four hours later, she found us. She'd gotten lost several times, but she had the mighty, mean metal hitch.

We needed a place to work to replace the old hitch with the new. Luckily, a U.S. Coast Guard station with a boat ramp was right next to the marina. The marina was small and used mainly for refueling, with no boat ramp. The fixed wooden pier was six feet higher than the Bumblebee. It would be impossible to remove the latch from the old missing hitch and reattach the new hitch. Someone would invariably fall into the cold water, and it was getting later in the afternoon. With a boat ramp, we could pull up and get off the Bumblebee and work on land.

We pushed the Bumblebees over to the Coast Guard station where we hoped to work. The station consisted of several low brick buildings slightly inshore with a few docks coming out to the water. A small white Coast Guard boat bobbed in the water near us. Several service people came over and talked with us, very nice and courteous, and we were likewise.

Then a Coast Guard guy came over. After all, the Coast Guard was there to help boaters in trouble, and we were in trouble. We just needed a little space on the boat ramp to reattach the new trailer hitch, and then we'd be on our way. I gave them my business card and explained what I was doing—the Great American Loop. But I was only 25 miles into the trip, so the idea didn't have much weight.

But then the big guy came over—brown Coast Guard baseball hat, blue parka, tall, balding, probably on his last tour of duty. He played by the book. He was there to show everybody who was in charge. We told him what we were doing.

"Is that our problem?" he asked.

I wondered what the pronoun "our" referred to. The government? The Coast Guard specifically? The species? I was about to inquire about that when he said, "This hitch isn't our problem. This is U.S. government property, and I want you off."

Could this guy know Jim? Could this be planned sabotage? Halflooper and I looked at each other with that same thought and simultaneously shook our heads no.

Confronted with the overwhelming power of such friendship, we thanked him and relocated back to the refueling marina, where we backed the Bumblebees back to back and started working on the trailer hitch. Halflooper held onto the dock to stabilize the jet skis. I held the jet skis together and worked on the trailer hitch at the same time. We cursed and strained and busted knuckles, but, finally, brute strength won out. The new hitch was in place. All looked well. The trailer was back in its spot behind the jet ski with the almighty, mean hitch.

The light was fading by then. It was already 4:30 p.m., so we decided to spend the night at a motel on Gwynn Island. We were in a small channel off the bay, not much of anything around, and the marina would be closing within the next half hour. The Island Motel was half a mile or so down the channel.

I turned the key to start my Bumblebee. Nothing. I tried again. Nothing. A new Bumblebee with less than 12 hours on it, and it was not starting. Was this a sign? How could the first day start out so badly? Did Jim have a voodoo Bumblebee?

Halflooper towed me to the motel, which was not officially open until the following day, May 25, but they were taking some guests who did not mind small inconveniences—like the restaurant not being open, which meant no food or beer. The Island Motel was a two story, built around 1950, with each room facing the west and the sunset over the water.

Well, this is fun, I thought as I lugged the bags up to the second-story room. Broken hitch, jet ski won't start, Coast Guard hospitality, no food, and no beer. Did I not make an appropriate sacrifice to the god of little annoying things that bug the hell out of you? I learned that what stops a person in his or her tracks when pursuing "dreams" may often not be the huge challenges but the small, tiresome breakdowns that aren't glamorous but are demanding and tax the patience. One huge wave could be tackled—either you survive or drown. It was the little waves that beat one after the other and slowly wore away the shoreline, those were the ones that should have their own appropriate deity, and I would offer said deity a beer, if I had one.

Then I walked into a room that had a gorgeous view of the small river that flowed around the motel. I immediately felt better. The clerk at the motel knew a fellow who worked on jet skis, even four-stroke jet skis, which were brand new to the market. He changed the spark plugs, and, yes, I was smart enough to have two extra sets with me. Sure enough, that was the problem. After the plug change, the Bumblebee started like a clock. I gave the gently humming jet ski a reassuring pat and asked it to please continue this new harmonious relationship without the constant need of a brand new spark plug each time I turned it off. Then the clerk at the motel offered to go back in the restaurant and get me a six pack of beer. That would take the chill off. Maybe the deity of small annoying problems had moved on to another unknowing wayfarer.

That evening I wondered whether the mishaps of the day were a sample of things to come. This was going to be a long trip. And, after all, why was I doing it? Maybe it wasn't a good idea. Did I want to spend weeks dealing with these sorts of things? I wanted adventure, the unknown, not the already-too-well-known breakdowns of the modern world. I thought that if fate could have found something more discouraging, it would have been hard. The physical challenge of being cold and drenched or even lost would have been more to my liking. If you met a foe, you wanted a great foe. But sometimes the greatest foe was just that—real and recognizable and just plain discouraging.

I remembered the remarks of friends when I had first mentioned my idea of doing the Great Loop on a jet ski. "Are you crazy?" "Can I take out life insurance on you?" Even later when they accepted the idea and their questions gave me possibilities to research (such as "Where do you fuel?"), there was still something in each set of eyes that refused to allow it as a reality. But then, with only 25 miles under my belt and so much trouble, none of it too glamorous, I wondered why I was doing it. Yes, I had planned every detail. Yes, I was prepared. But no one could be prepared for everything. What would happen out there on the water? Would I wish it were only a broken trailer hitch and a wet spark plug? I had created my own monster, the Great Loop. Did I really have it in me to do it?

Right before I left, a reporter from the local newspaper had asked to interview me about the trip. It had gone well. She said the story would be published that week. That week, the whole community would be reading about it. I couldn't turn back, dragging my tail between my legs with people saying, "You dumb ass." I couldn't face that, but right then the trip was very real and very dangerous. I wasn't at all sure why I was doing it or whether I could. After all, I was 50 and had spent years in an office. I was no athlete. But, I thought, nobody told you to do it. You wanted to do it. And you still want to.

I tried to get warm by rubbing a towel on my legs and arms, and then I put on some dry clothes. Most of the clothes were wet. I opened a beer and avoided Halflooper's gaze. He knew this was a long way from what I had hoped for on the first day. If nothing else, I thought we would be pulling onshore for the night at least 140 miles into the trip, with jovial tales of great sights and terrific moments.

The motel clerk called the room to tell us that there was a local restaurant open. We made our way over to the Seabreeze Restaurant, about a quarter mile down the road. With a couple beers under our belts, we walked through the deep green countryside of Gywnns Island.

The Seabreeze was no bigger than an apartment and had 10 tables, no alcohol, and no credit cards. I asked the owner, about 70 years old, why he didn't serve alcohol. "We get people in here drinking and they'll take the table for the whole night," he said.

"Why no credit cards?" I asked.

"Because I don't have to."

"Are you afraid you'll lose business?"

"I got more business than I got room to seat people. Why should I take a credit card when I have to pay the bank to accept it? Hey, nothing like cash."

The conversation, fresh seafood, and homemade dessert revived our spirits.

The view from the windows was wonderful. The light of the late-day sky flooded over the water, reminding me of what I so loved about the water and always had. The sky faded pink and deep red. The waves lapped into the nearby shore, shallow and restful. Nearby, a flock of birds lifted off and took to the sky. An old unused series of logs that had once held up a pier still stood upright out into the water, precisely placed like monuments to a forgotten, primitive religion.

It was a full, luscious moment. It was a moment I didn't expect. I thought I'd be tired and discouraged and probably fighting to keep my spirits up. I had felt that way just a few hours earlier. But it had all changed. The moment captured me.

I had spent my life planning for the future, avoiding mistakes, anticipating anything that could go wrong, and trying to be sure it didn't. I had been tied to the constant demand of the future. I had worked hard for security and achievement. I had those. But I had missed a lot of these moments.

I didn't miss that one. It sank into me. The trip was worth it.

Of course I was going to continue. I was still a disciple of the water and the unknown and the personal test.

The light glowed over the nearby reeds. I didn't know what the next day would bring on the water. And that was great.

"How's your butt?" Ed asked. Riding a jet ski all day put a strain on the rear.

"Don't ask. How's yours?"

"My butt hurts."

"You think Jim is really taking bets that I can't finish this trip?" I asked.

"I guess," Ed replied, finishing another piece of homemade pie. "I think I'm going to bet," he said.

I wondered which way he would bet. I couldn't blame him if it was against me.

Chapter 3
On My Own

The next day Halflooper and I were out on the pier and were caulking and repairing the water trailer.

Halflooper had taken a break to talk on the cell phone. He suddenly put it down and said, "The odds are up!"

"What odds?" This trailer seemed to want more water inside than outside.

"Jim's. The bet. You're at 22 to one now."

"Mom will be happy. More money for her."

"Maybe Jim heard about yesterday," Halflooper said.

"No way. How could he know about that? And why would he be upping the odds so early on?" Why was he? The more I thought about it, the more annoyed I got, and I was damned tired of caulking. He could make it 500 to one. I was going to finish the damned trip, with or without a water trailer.

"So what happens if this trailer busts?" Halflooper asked.

"That's it. No more trailer."

The following day, we left Gwynn Island and were back out on the Chesapeake, heading around the Great American Loop. Halflooper was running ahead of me on his jet ski because the trailer, as usual, was slowing me down. But I was still able to maintain about 35 miles per hour. I was taking the waves as usual. The jet ski would go up as the trailer was coming down and vice versa. I came down off a wave, and the trailer came unhitched and just died there in the water, about 50 yards behind me. I circled back, looking at the annoying little thing bobbing around on the waves. That was it. Two strikes, you're out!

Halflooper doubled back and circled the trailer with me and suggested we push it out farther a ways and hit it with the flare gun. "Target practice," he said.

The idea had appeal, particularly because there were about 10 gallons of gas tied to the thing. It would go up like fireworks. I relished the idea of that leaky little trailer blazing up across the water accompanied by a big boom.

But we weren't that far from the Gwynn Island Coast Guard station. I then imagined our friendly Coast Guard commander coming up to us again with his usual affable greeting.

"No," I said, "let's tow it in."

So into the Annapolis Marina we went. It was a bright sunny day, but I was very tired of dealing with the trailer. So was Halflooper. We towed the trailer into the marina. Annapolis had a wonderful harbor made up mainly of sailboaters and the U.S. Naval Academy. The marinas there were first class. You could smell big dollars and big boats. There were all types of boats, more than a hundred. It was a parking lot for money. Most of the large boats had major algae growing under the bottom of the hulls. Those boats hadn't been out of harbor in years. That's what happened with boating. First, there was the excitement of owning the boat and then, finally, the "For Sale" sign hanging off the rail.

There on the busy dock was where we met Tim, the dock boy.

"Tim," I said, "would you like to have this trailer?"

"Sure." He still wasn't sure what I wanted in return. His eternal soul or free tickets to the local rock show?

"I'll make a deal," I said. "You get rid of any of the stuff I don't want, and you can have it."

"It's a deal," he readily accepted. He had rosy cheeks and a cheerful charm, probably the result of spending his days outside with the water.

How I wished I still had a real boat where I used to complain about storage room. I hadn't known what luxury was.

The famous Facsuets Boat Supply store was right around the corner from the marina, so Halflooper and I walked there to look for some storage alternative for the jet ski. We went up and down the well-stocked aisles and decided out coolers, backpacks, and any other container we could spot. We pulled them out, studied them, and then looked at each other and shook our heads, "Nope." Finally I spotted two pieces of luggage. They were top-quality, water-resistant, and zip top, and they had a water liner inside to hold or resist water. I could tie them on the jet ski with bungee cords.

Halflooper looked dubious.

"What?" I asked.

"A beautiful new jet ski with two Jed Clampet bags attached to the side?"

I pointed out their key attribute again, "Water resistant!"

Back on the dock, I separated the items I needed from those I didn't. The most important items were those needed for safety such as charts, a flare kit, tools, extra parts for the Bumblebee, and some clothes. It was a painful process. And frustrating. I had already eliminated so many things for the small storage space of the trailer, and there I was reducing "essentials" again. But I did manage to keep a lucky wooden nickel from the pile Halflooper thought I should toss.

So we left Tim on the dock with a hearty goodbye, which he returned. I hoped he would enjoy the trailer and my pup tent.

Then we headed into the Chesapeake and Delaware Canal, known as the C&D. The canal emptied into the Chesapeake on one side and the Delaware Bay on the other. It was a man-made sea level canal about 20 feet deep and 100 feet wide, built to accommodate seagoing vessels. Since it was first excavated back in the early 1800s, it had gone through a constant series of expansions to make it both deeper and wider. Six large bridges crossed the canal, and there were hiking and bicycle trails along the shoreline.

When we hit the canal, the wind had changed, coming from the north 10 to 15 miles per hour, with waves running two to three feet. It was raining. Heading into the north, we were feeling the change. It was a working canal built for big industrial ships, not jet skis or recreational vehicles, and that's what it felt like. The water was murky and sluggish and shallow, and the currents could be tricky. It was not a place where you wanted to go swimming.

The main action on the canal was at Chesapeake City, where the recreational boats gathered for socializing and a bite to eat. All of the boats were power crafts and mainly from the Baltimore area, out for the day and enjoying the waters of the canal. We rode as we always did when we were in close proximity of other boaters, on the right side of the canal, maybe 15 feet from the shoreline. Halflooper was following my wake, maybe 30 feet behind. After all, with the trailer gone, I was able to zip along about 35 to 40 miles per hour. Large boulders onshore kept the water from the mainland. It was nice to be riding on calm water with no waves other than those from our fellow boaters.

A tugboat came by pulling a big black oil tanker. Halflooper and I gave them plenty of room. It was hard to believe shallow water could hold up all those tons of crude oil and metal or that it could be pulled by one line going to the tugboat. The tug kept a steady pace, and the huge tanker behind it floated with small effort. I saw no signs of human life on the tanker, which gave it a sort of sci-fi quality. I could barely spot the captain of the tugboat behind the front window of his ship. I wondered how many times a day he did this and how long he had done it and whether he was the only person in control of so much power floating across 100 feet of water. I had been on the C&D Canal before but never when a tug was coming through. From four feet off the water and that close, it looked as if a building were moving down the canal. All that black metal had an eerie quality.

Midpoint in the C&D was Chesapeake City. We stopped and went to a B&B—Inn at the Canal. It was a beautiful Victorian home, well maintained, with friendly owners and a view of the canal and the harbor.

I called my wife. She asked, "So, how's the C&D?"

"Beautiful," I fibbed. I wasn't going to say anything negative to her yet about the trailer or the trip. "But you'd really love this B&B. Did you hear anything about this bet Jim's got going?"

"Oh, that," she laughed. "I don't think he's serious."

"He's taking real money."

"I'm sure he isn't," she said. She knew a bet would only fire me on.

"No, probably not," I agreed. But I had a strong feeling Jim was taking real money. Mom said he took her real money. But the idea of a bet would only unsettle my wife further, so I decided to drop the subject.

The next day, Halflooper and I were out on the C&D, heading toward the Delaware Bay. I had traveled that route before on a 42-foot motor yacht. I knew that the farther south we went on the Delaware River, the rougher the water would get as the wind blew in from the south. We passed the Salem Nuclear Power Plant, so large it must have been visible from 20 miles off. The haystack tower bellowed out clouds of smoke over the canal. If the Bumblebee felt small by the tanker, it felt even smaller going by that plant.

Salem Nuclear Plant looms in the distance.

Below the Salem plant, the Delaware began to open up into the Delaware Bay, which in turn led back into the Atlantic. We followed the green and red buoys of the ship channel. Occasionally a big lighthouse designated a navigational hazard. The water was salty. Delaware Bay got wider and wider going south. Soon we couldn't see land from out on the water. The water temperature was dropping because we were getting closer to the mouth of the river, which flowed into the Atlantic Ocean, where the waves increased in height.

The game plan was to head east, toward the Jersey coast, looking for land and fuel. Following the coastline, you used a lot more fuel because the land jutted in and out, in what seemed like a half-moon shape, but those half-moons were five to 10 miles around. Often we thought we had reached the tip of the half-moon only to discover it jutted out even farther, following a long curve. The GPS showed a straight line, but the visible horizon was water and water and miles of it. I often wondered whether the GPS was wrong.

The lower Delaware had few places to hide from the bad weather or water and few marinas. After several attempts, we found Money

Island Marina, about halfway to Cape May on the Delaware River. It was very, very small. Refueling the jet skis required two people: one to put the fuel in and the other to fan away the "flying teeth"—small biting insects, ferociously discontent that Money Island wasn't all they'd hoped for. They bit like crazy, and they were everywhere. We swatted and yelled and cursed, and, as soon as we could, Halflooper and I raced to the small marina hut with the flying teeth right behind us.

We stepped into a gray building, which was decorated with a 10-foot plastic shark and buoys that dangled like jewelry near the door. Inside, there was a group of local fishermen sitting by the wood-burning stove and chewing tobacco. They were a rough- looking group but seemed to go with the unkempt marina. They stopped talking when Halflooper and I came in. The silence was thick. You could see what they thought—city slickers coming into their waters. Afraid of bugs.

The young blonde woman behind the counter greeted us, used to seeing grown humans in full flight from the insects. I chatted with the woman and handed her one of my greeting cards. It explained who I was and told her about the Great Loop adventure I was undertaking.

Our greeter and ice breaker at Money Island Marina

She stood behind the desk by the cash register and read it with a strangely serious preoccupation. I wondered whether I'd misspelled something on the card.

She looked up and said, "Wait a second," and then stepped into a back room.

When she left, the deadly silence returned with the fishermen. I tried to break the ice by asking, "How far to Cape May Ferry?"

No reply.

She returned with a piece of paper with the handwriting: "Chicago to Chicago, John Moffett 5/9/00. 36 years old."

John Moffett had been there! What were the chances that I'd come to that out-of-place marina, just as he had? I was following in his footsteps. It was definitely wonderful. I tried to pump our hostess for more information, but she couldn't remember that much about him.

"How long did he stop?" I asked.

"Not long," she replied

Suddenly the fishermen were interested. The ice melted.

"You're coming all the way from Virginia Beach?" one asked.

"Yes, all the way," I affirmed.

"Well, shit, man, that's a trip." They were impressed. They had never gone more than 10 miles either way on the Delaware River. It turned into a great time with the local fishermen, talking and sharing stories and information.

With 35 miles to go while there was still daylight, Halflooper and I said our farewells to the Money Island Marina folk. The flying teeth pursued us all the way back to our jet skis.

The wind was out of the south at 10 miles per hour, creating two-foot waves. The waves held us at about 35 to 45 miles per hour. After an hour, I signaled to Halflooper, and we pulled over in a cove to take a break and talk about the rest of the trip. Cape May was coming up, and I knew Halflooper had to turn back there. The cove was another one of those half-moons, but it was calm water. We were about 100 feet offshore with little or no activity. Waterfront homes lined the shore, one after the other.

Halflooper sat on his jet ski with that "I want to continue" look on his face. I didn't know what was on my face. Probably panic. I wished Halflooper could keep going with me. I knew he couldn't. He had a job to get back to, and he couldn't be away any longer.

"I'll have to leave up here," Halflooper said, meaning Cape May. "You think you got that Bumblebee's problem solved?"

"Sure. No problems now." It would only be worse if I made him worry.

We talked about other possible problems and what we'd been through so far. Halflooper was a good friend. I would miss him. I guess it showed in my face because we both got a little sentimental. We'd been through a lot together, not just with these few days, but with all the planning and testing for the trip. He had to go back then, and I dearly wished he didn't have to. He was a friend of 30 years, and the past few months had made our bond even deeper.

But we were also men and couldn't take the "warm fuzzy" that long.

"Hey, when you get back, would you do me a favor and get your own damned toothbrush?"

"Did I even ask to borrow yours?" he said.

"Man, you need a toothbrush."

"They're pearly white!" he grinned to demonstrate and fired up his jet ski. I wondered whether he had been using my toothbrush after all. Some things were better not known.

We headed out of the cove and down to Cape May. We stopped at the Miss Crisp Marina, where a guy gave us a ride to the local motel. Mr. Bob was scheduled to drive up to Cape May with a trailer, and Halflooper would return with him. Mr. Bob was a friend (and I could spell his name backward and forward, B-O-B) who loved to drive, hence the trip there. He was a CPA by day and by night a long-haul truck driver wannabe.

Mr. Bob was there as scheduled.

The motel was one story, built in the 1950s. I unpacked. I was cold and wet, and it was nice to get out of the wet suit, shower, and put on some dry clothes. Or damp clothes. The bags were 50 percent wet. Again, I had to remove all the items to dry them. I was trying to get this down to a routine because I knew it would happen every time I came off the water. I had my own metal lawn chair on the walkway where the sun was shining and where I hung a few of my goods out to dry. I gathered a few more lawn chairs and put all the wet items out to dry.

I needed a beer. When I asked the motel clerk where to get one, he said, "There's not enough people here to get a beer."

Huh?

He explained. A township needed a certain population before it could sell beer. That township was short.

"So you don't have enough people to have a beer?" Mr. Bob asked.

"That's right."

"Well, who does?"

"You need a population of 5,000, I think. Or is it six?"

"Well, where is there such a population of 5,000 or more?" Bob asked.

We got directions. We went off to find the exact demographics required for a beer in New Jersey. Soon after, we found a bar selling beer.

"I hope nobody moves," Ed said.

"Or dies in the next two hours," Mr. Bob added.

The next morning at 8:00 Halflooper and I walked to our separate jet skis. That was when he went his way and I went mine. He fired up his jet ski. I tried to do the same. But nothing happened. Again. My jet ski just bobbed in the water, dead as a duck decoy. I tried again.

"You buy new things so this doesn't happen," I muttered.

"This happens to all new things," Halflooper contradicted.

"Since when?" I kept pushing the ignition button.

"Years."

"Well, shit. This is Japanese made. It doesn't happen to Japanese made."

"That's a kind of narrow way of thinking."

"I paid $10,000 for this! Hmmm . . . the Friday Lemon Law," I said woefully.

"It's a test model. You're part of the great experiment. Work out the bugs. Be part of the Yamaha experience, good buddy."

"If this is a test model, they should have to pay me."

"Let's tow you down to the ramp."

Halflooper hooked up a line from his jet ski to mine and then towed me and the jet ski to the nearest ramp. Mr. Bob pulled up with his trailer, and we took the Bumblebee to Pier 47 in Wildwood, New Jersey.

At the dealership, they let me watch while they checked it out. Then they called the Mother Country (Yamaha's main office). Yamaha had been following the progress with the new four-stroke jet ski.

"I feel better knowing that," I said to the repairman.

"So do I," he agreed. But to be on the safe side, he wanted to keep the jet ski one more day to give it a test run and check it out.

I agreed, though mentally I had started to calculate the days lost to the trailer and then the jet ski. I had only so many days to make the Great Loop. Granted it was still late May and there were months of summer left, but it was another 5,000-plus miles, and I'd really only begun the trip. I couldn't afford these constant breakdowns. I'd never make it around the Loop while the weather was good if I lost one day out of three to mechanical failures. Was this another sign that I should have given it up right then? I pushed the thought away. It was too early in the trip to be writing it off. And soon I'd lose the fun of having Halflooper around. But, no, Jim wasn't going to get the satisfaction or my mother's money.

Halflooper and Mr. Bob dropped me off at a motel on the boardwalk of Wildwoods. I waved goodbye to both. Unloading again at this motel, I discovered that all my introductory cards were wet. I laid them out, all 500, one by one in the hallway to dry. Just as I put the last one down, a wind came up and sent dozens flying. Off I went chasing them. It seemed to somehow fit the theme of the day. (Later, those cards would prove more valuable than I might have thought then, so the chase was well worth it.)

With all the cards finally dry, I decided to go check out the amusement park, located right by the ocean. It was like Coney Island in the 1950s. The three huge Ferris wheels and the roller coaster came right out to the sand. There was a long, wide boardwalk with shops and restaurants and benches. The whole thing sort of looked like an elaborate modern sculpture by the shore—swirls of metal, towers of red steel, whirling cars that zoomed by with a merry lack of direction.

Against the sea, an amusement park had a self-contradictory quality—that great indifferent, eternal body of water lapped at the feet of these huge toys for adults and children. The toys distracted and amused and collected crowds like a magnet. The waves kept lapping in no matter how fast the rides went, and it left a mixed feeling—a sense of abandon and freedom from everyday lives of work and hassles to a childlike world full of amazing new toys and then the waves out there, promising real freedom. But it was fun to walk around the rides,

Wildwood Amusement Park

up and down the boardwalk, nod to the others also enjoying the day and the amusements.

Late in the day, the mood seemed to change among the people I met on the boardwalk. Something had happened out on the water, and word was just spreading. It involved some local people. Three young brothers were dead, drowned at sea. They'd all been together in a 36-foot cigarette speedboat, which could go up to 100 miles per hour. The brothers didn't have their life vests on. The life vests were found in the boat, which was towed into shore. Local officials speculated that the boat must have capsized about a mile out from the beach. You couldn't survive out there in the water long without protection, much less no life vest. The divers had been called in and hadn't found them. Were the brothers going too fast and hit that odd wave? Were they horsing around as brothers do? The real answers to why would probably never be known. I looked past the roller coaster to the ocean. Three brothers, gone, so quickly, without explanation.

God be with them.

I had 5,350 miles to go in something one-third the size and nowhere near the weight of a cigarette boat. My day in the Atlantic was coming up.

The next morning, I was at Pier 47 and the dealership, the first of many to come. So what had gone wrong with my jet ski? The Mother Country didn't know. How was water getting into the combustion chamber? I decided to talk to the Mother Country myself. I explained my trip around the Great Loop and that this was not how I envisioned the start of the trip. The woman I spoke to reassured me that the Mother Country was keeping track of every service call in detail and by serial number.

"I feel better knowing that," I said.

"So do I," said the repairman.

Neither one of us had a clue as to why the jet ski hadn't started the previous day. But Mother was watching. Of that we were certain and very reassured. Would they pull out their satellite lens and study me as

I zoomed off the Atlantic coast? I felt certain they would at least try. I had a new friend or at least not an enemy.

By then it was almost noon, and I wanted to get going. I brought the jet ski back and repacked. I went to attach the GPS, and there was no mounting bracket. I searched through my few possessions again. It wasn't there. Without the mounting bracket, I would have to hold the GPS in my hand. I called the previous two motels where I had stayed, but they didn't find it. I called Halflooper and asked that he pick one up from the local marine store and ship it to a destination a few days farther on. I knew the way, by instinct and the water markers, but I needed the GPS out so it would record the mileage that I was covering. Moffett hadn't had a GPS, and I wanted an accurate reading of the miles.

Then I hit the water. I wouldn't be out long because I got started so late in the day. But I wanted my first day alone to be one spent on the water, not in the repair shop at the dealership. It was May 29, five days into the trip, and I was heading from Cape May, New Jersey, to Somers Point, New Jersey. I was riding in a canal that paralleled the Atlantic Ocean. The canal was protected from the Atlantic Ocean waves that pounded the shoreline. The weather was sunny, about 65 degrees, and the wind was blowing 25 to 30 miles per hour from the north, but I was protected from the mighty Atlantic Ocean by the canal. It was one of those days that anybody who had a watercraft wanted to be out enjoying the day. The haze of late day blurred the line between the water and the sky. The drone of the jet ski and the vibration under my feet as I skimmed the water were steady and reassuring. I was going about 35 to 45 miles per hour most of the time.

My nerves were on edge despite the beautiful day and quiet, calm run. The jet ski had broken down on me twice. Would it do it again? Would I have a craft I could depend on from then on? Could I depend on it then? Without Halflooper running with me, I wasn't so sure I was that much safer than those young boys who had drowned. I was out there on my own, and it was up to me to figure it out if anything unexpected happened. What if I hit something and fell off? What if the unit broke down? How long would I survive in the water? Would I find the next stop or miss it?

The saltwater was burning my eyes again. Halflooper wore goggles, but I never did. I wanted to be able to see all the way around me. I wanted to see what was in the water—pilings, trash, plastic bags that could be sucked into the intake.

My hands were throbbing with the cold of holding the GPS and the throttle.

I thought about the three lost brothers back at Wildwood. Like me, they had probably just loved the water and were out to have fun on such a bright, sunny day. But the ocean with 30-mile-per-hour winds was not like that amusement park with people all around and hundreds of safety checks. I understood why they loved speed on the water. So did I. I loved the jet ski riding the top of the waves, the views, the air in my lungs, and the sense of taking flight into boundless space. How could three young men have not been able to get back to their boat? Whatever happened, it must have been in seconds.

Then I thought seriously of giving up the whole adventure. I was taking a lot of unnecessary risk. It was one thing to do this in a boat, but on a jet ski? Apparently even a 36-foot boat wasn't safe out there. Who was I kidding? Without Halflooper, I was running a serious risk out there alone.

A seagull flew up, and the sun flickered off the water.

I hadn't known the brothers, but I did know the lure of speed and water, and I, too, could easily forget the dangers. I tried to stay alert to all the possibilities out there—hitting something in the water, the jet ski just shutting off on me, an unexpected wave. But at times, there was something about the drone of the jet ski and the distances that could shift your focus away—just as you could drive 70 or 80 miles per hour on the freeway and stop thinking about the thousands that die each day on America's highways, stop worrying whether a tire would blow or what's around the next turn or what fool was going to jump the dividing lane. Of course we didn't think of all that. We enjoyed the ride. So did I.

The trip was like a long weekend, only this time I didn't have to get back on Sunday night to make sure I got a good night's sleep before Monday morning at the office. This time there was no Monday morning at the office or the sinking feeling that sometimes came on Sunday afternoon—it was all over so quickly, and did I really want to sit under florescent lights again and listen to the phones ringing all day? (Of course a part of me relished that because it was my work and I was good at it, but a part of me didn't.) Now I was free. And I loved it. "Every day is Saturday."

The air was crisp and slightly cool off the water. Some clouds began to cover the sun; it was not a good feeling, with the water temperature about 55 degrees. I skirted the eastern shoreline. There were sailboats out and a few fishing boats. I was following the green markers in the water. They bobbed up about every two or three miles. The number written on the marker corresponded to a number on a chart, though you couldn't always be sure a marker was correct. They moved around out there. They weren't like street signs that stayed in one place.

I turned my attention to all the details of the trip that I knew I had to keep covered. I was going through the mental tally of what I'd need for the rest of the trip, trying not to forget something. Small mistakes led to disaster. Batteries. Next set of charts for Mom to send. What about gloves? Batteries. I took out the notepad in the compartment and wrote down my list. It was a trick to write with a pen on a piece of paper while traveling at 35 miles per hour. The notes always looked like pig scratch, but I could make them out.

As I looked up, a bird's foot was about six inches from my face. I ducked and swerved. The seagull dropped the fish in its mouth and pooped at the same time. We missed each other by inches. What was wrong with that bird! Didn't it hear me coming? What kind of a self-respecting bird just sits there in midair, miles of empty space around it, and lets a man run right into it? What a way to go! For both of us.

Collision wipes out bird and man somewhere off coast of southern New Jersey. No details available. But Yamaha regrets the incident.

After I calmed down again, I realized that the bird probably hadn't heard me coming. It was intent on catching a late lunch. If the wind was coming at you, you couldn't hear a four-stroke Bumblebee coming up from behind. I wiped the poop off my shoulder. Well, as they say, "Shit happens."

An hour or so later, I came into Somers Point and docked right at the waterfront motel. Pier 4 Motel was a modern four-story high-rise with "PIER 4" in large block letters across the roof. They prided themselves on having the "friendliest staff in town." I shuddered to think what the second-friendliest staff in town was like. The manager must have been having a bad day. He was not what I call the stellar greeter master. He frowned when he saw me, wet suit on, hauling the Jed Clampet bags. He frowned when he took the damp credit card. He wiped it off before he swiped it as though he suspected I had pissed on it. I was still in my wet suit and said the obvious, "Water."

"Water?" he said suspiciously.

"Saltwater," I specified.

Water was dripping from my feet, and he just wanted me out of his lobby. He grumbled when he gave me the room key, and I grumbled back. Hey, this was New Jersey. Grumble for grumble. He seemed to relax a little. I knew and understood the rituals of Jersey. All was well in the universe.

In truth, the exchange wasn't amusing or pleasant. However, I didn't let it get me down, though it didn't quite lift me up. I still had to dry out all my stuff. A good meal helped lift my spirits.

I congratulated myself on my first day alone out on the water. Raising my beer, I saluted the seagull I had narrowly missed. May you live to catch fish and poop another day, friend. And may we never meet again.

Back at the motel, I decided to check my e-mail. I hadn't before because the signal had been out of range. And, until then, I didn't think I had much to e-mail to anybody. Luck! I was in range and had seven messages waiting. They included: "Are you cold?" "Where are you now?" "How's your butt?"

I smiled and tapped in my reply message.

```
From: <waverider4222@palm.com>

Date: Wed, 29 May 2002 03:06:24 +0000 (GMT)

To: all@all.com

Hello ALL,,,,,moving along,,,,finished the shake
down part of the cruise,,Chesapeake Bay,,,,yes
it was rough water every day,,,now in Cape May
NJ,,,moving to calm waters ,,headed to New York
City,,,having a blast,,,lost the water trailer
outside of Anopolis,,,gave it to a dock boy
named Tim,,made his day,,,had to downsize big
time,,,,but it was a good thing,,,,wish all was
here,,,I would buy the beer, would help the pop-
ulation in Jersey,,,,talk later

Larry[1]
```

After the e-mail, I called my wife. It was good to hear her voice.

"How was it without Ed?" she asked.

"A great day," I said.

"No problems?"

"Absolutely none." Note: We didn't mention the feet of birds or a jet ski that wouldn't start, not to a woman who hated the combination of engines and water and who was worried and ready to jump on anything to get me home again.

"That's wonderful." She did sound relieved.

I asked her about her day at the bank. She was still working there, heading up the transition. I understood the problems. I'd had 30 years

[1]All e-mails were composed by tapping keys on a cell phone, with no keyboard or spell-checker. For authenticity, they appear as originally written.

of dealing with them. I offered some suggestions on why the check-capture machine had gone down. Oddly, I missed Ms. Boeing and the job for a while.

But not for long.

The next day I would be back out heading up the Jersey shore into New York Harbor. I anticipated that more than I missed the job. I couldn't wait to be on the water again. What would I see? Who would I meet? There was danger out there, but there was life out there too, and Larry and his Bumblebee were out to experience it, and experience it we would.

If the jet ski started in the morning, that would be a great day had by all. Knock on wood!

Chapter 4
New Waters: New Jersey through the Erie Canal

That day I was starting to get into waters I had never traveled. The first day of that leg of the trip—Somers Point to Manasquan Inlet—was rough, with winds out of the north 15 to 20 miles per hour. The ride was slow and bouncy. But at the first stop, a lovely young woman named Michelle came out to the dock to greet me and filled up the Bumblebee for me. It was a fixed wooden dock, and fueling was hard, so I appreciated the gesture. I had just had four hard hours on the water, and I was feeling lonely and tired.

She was not the exception on the trip. Often, when I was down, I would pick up my e-mail and be surprised to find that another person had joined the trip. It got me through a lot of bad times—just knowing all those friends were out there in cyberspace following my journey, wanting to be a part of it, wishing they also could go. It would remind me of how lucky I was to be on the trip.

The stretch from Somers Point, New Jersey, to Buffalo, New York, had the quality of a pleasant tune, without the serious extremes that would follow on Lake Erie itself.

June 1, moving into Manasquan Inlet, I had to go through Point Pleasant Canal. I had just entered when I was pulled over by the New Jersey Water Patrol. No jet skis allowed, he said. He called in my registration numbers to check me out.

"Well," I said, "since there's only one way into Manasquan Inlet, I guess we've got a problem."

"There's only one solution," he said. I had to call Boat Tow U.S. They would tow me through the canal.

"If that's the only way, let's go," I said.

Boat Tow showed up and tied me to the towline, and off we went. I had a greater chance of tipping this way than if I'd ridden it alone. But I did get tow insurance for the whole country, something I hadn't thought of before.

Once I got to the other side and the tow took off, the U.S. Coast Guard pulled me over. By this time, I was not a happy camper.

"What do you guys want?" I asked.

"Nothing. We just wanted to see with our own eyes a jet ski registered from Virginia in these parts of the water."

They had been listening over the VHF when the New Jersey Water Patrol called to check my registration.

Lots of big ears out there!

That night at the marina, I sat at the bar and had a few beers. That was where I met Brian. We got acquainted, and I explained my trip around the Great American Loop.

"Do you want a sponsor?" he asked.

"Sure," I replied, surprised.

Brian's company, Extreme Offshore Fishing Company, would be my first and only sponsor. Brian said he would pay for 500 miles of fuel if I wore his company T-shirt.

"A deal," I said.

"One catch," he said. "You've got to make it to St. Augustine, Florida, first."

"I appreciate your sponsorship, Brian," I said.

We shook hands.

I took his e-mail and told him I'd let him know where to send the T-shirt. Hmm, I wondered whether he would.

The next morning I was up early. That day was going to be a challenge. I was going out into the Atlantic and into New York Harbor and then up the Hudson River. First I had breakfast and then listened to the VHF weather report. It was looking good—west winds five to 10 miles per hour in the morning.

Coming out of the Manasquan Inlet, I couldn't have asked for a more beautiful day. The wind was coming out of the west. It was perfect. The ocean was flat and calm, with swells of only two to three feet.

At the same moment that my spirit leaped up with the glory of the day, my hands and face felt the cold. It was freezing! I was still holding that GPS, and my fingers were throbbing. All I had on were cotton gloves. I put the GPS between my legs. Even though it was a pain to put on, I was wearing the wet suit. With those kinds of temperatures, I had no choice. When the water splashed up over me, the shock of the cold was startling. But there wouldn't be any wet suit gloves until Troy, New York, where Mom was sending them. My 85-year-old mother, known as Hip Bee on the Internet, was part of my three-person ground support crew.

Aside from the cold water, the run from Manasquan Inlet to Sandy Point, New Jersey, was perfect. As I rounded Sandy Point, I hit heavy west winds; it was choppy and not pretty, with lots of junk in the water and lots of boaters. The waters around Sandy Point were congested, even though there was no commercial marina for 15 miles in any direction. Boats were not allowed onshore, but the offshore water was jammed with them. Fishermen had their poles in the water. Sailboats floated by. Yachts. Party boats. Many of the residents of these boats had their binoculars fixed on the Bumblebee and me. As I went by, I could read the expression in their faces: "Where in the hell is this jet ski from, and how did he get here?" Such puzzled disapproval never made me blink. But from their point of view, I must have looked suspicious. It wasn't long after 9/11, and there I was—in a black wet suit, with a dark tan from days on the water, appearing out of nowhere. To reassure people, I always waved, even if they didn't always wave back, but they usually did. But now that I think about it, maybe those binoculars were focused on the nude beach at Sandy Point.

The run into New York Harbor was quite awesome. I came in under the high Verrazano Bridge that swung out from Brooklyn to Staten Island. The heavy traffic of the city dotted the roads, barely visible from the water. The harbor opened up, big and decorated with all those great well-known symbols. I went by Ellis Island, gateway to the United States, restored, looking official but not really functional in the sense of an operating bureaucracy of today. As I came into the harbor, the

The ever-classic Staten Island Ferry

Standing proud, the Statue of Liberty

Statue of Liberty didn't seem that big, particularly set against the New York City skyline. But as I approached, the lady revealed her glory—gracious, strong, well balanced, the strong arm holding the torch skyward, the Apollo-like features both noble and intelligent. Less than a year after 9/11, the familiar skyline of New York City was, of course, changed. It was hard to identify the skyline as that of New York, and the effect was in a way disorienting. Without the Twin Towers looming over lower Manhattan, the skyline seemed more like that of any other major U.S. city—still impressive but not distinctly New York. That empty air where the towers had been seemed painful to look at, though I had not known New York as the millions who lived there had. But it was still a great city at the edge of the continent, with the famous Empire State Building spiking to the sky and the old orange ferry pushing its commuters to Staten Island.

It was rough water in the harbor—lots of chop and waves from every direction. Most of it was coming from the number of crafts in the water—ships, ferries, and the Coast Guard, with a machine gun mounted on the front and manned. As I passed the city, I glanced down the long canyons between the towering buildings. Out on the water I could not hear the horns and motors or feel the thousands crowded on the sidewalks. But if there was a lot of traffic on those streets, there was also a lot of traffic out on the water. I took as many pictures as I could. At the next stop, I would send the film off to Tim, the guy running the Web site for the trip, so he could post the pictures on the Internet. But I didn't stop. I had been to New York before, and I had a date in Tarrytown. Coming in past lower Manhattan, I veered a little to the left and moved toward the mighty Hudson rolling down the west side of the island.

I moved by all the famous landmarks. I came under the Washington Bridge and up the Hudson, a wide river with steep grades above New York. Tarrytown was a big suburb just north of New York City. The commuters took the train from there down to the city. They drove to the train station, got on the train, rode into the city, and returned that afternoon. I felt doubly lucky.

In Tarrytown, I learned about yacht clubs. Yes, I had heard of yacht clubs but was not familiar with them. In the South, we had country clubs mainly for golf and docks for the boating enthusiasts. But in this neck of the woods, the yacht club was the organization for those in love with boating—specifically this was the Hudson River Yacht Club. They had all the amenities of the country club but no golf course.

But if it had been rough coming through the New York Harbor and the "lookers" at Sandy Point hadn't seemed that friendly, these people were great and very interested in my adventure. They welcomed me as if I were a visiting dignitary.

"Where did you say you started?" a young man asked.

"Virginia Beach."

"Virginia?" He looked surprised.

"Yes." I smiled.

"Welcome, stranger! You've come a long way."

I guess the saying held true—if you originated more than 50 miles from the area you were in, you were the outsider. But they didn't make me feel like an outsider. I spent a good part of the evening talking with those interested boaters.

I was beginning to notice something that I had never noted before about boaters, possibly because I hadn't left my own waters for that long and not nearly for this kind of distance. Most boaters and marina folk had never strayed more than 50 miles from their home port. Usually they had gone about 15 miles from their home base. This was very odd to me. Most of the time when I would stop at various marinas, they would advise me on what was upstream, but it was not too far upstream. They simply had never traveled farther than that.

I was the exception to that rule. I had made long trips before on the water, but it was mostly in the South, along the eastern shoreline. I hadn't been that far north on the water. I was moving out of the waters and climate that I knew. The unknown had a lure and a danger to it. I had felt fairly confident, until now, that I knew the water and was fairly certain of what I would encounter, even in New York Harbor. I had prepared myself for that. But from then on, it was going to be new. I had left home—that was for sure.

The next day, June 2, I headed straight up the Hudson River to Kingston, New York. The wind was coming straight down the Hudson at 15 to 20 miles per hour. When I went by a power plant, I steered the Bumblebee far to the other side. Realizing that I probably looked like a terrorist in my wet suit, I didn't want to get security nervous. The countryside along the Hudson was green and lush most of the way. It was a beautiful spring day. I ran at 40 miles per hour all day until I reached Kingston, New York.

I got into Kingston early, about 11 a.m. Kingston was a beautiful old historic river port town. When I arrived—it was a Sunday—there were police boats all over the waterfront. The night before, Saturday, a lot of partiers had been on the water. A gentleman had fallen over the side of a boat, and nobody realized he was missing until the next morning. It was a middle-of-the-night drowning. The police were trying to locate the body. I talked to the local water patrol, and he said that it was very normal and that it happened frequently during the summer season, particularly during a holiday weekend.

Historical Kingston was a great little city, lots of small stores, restaurants, and river history. One restaurant in particular got my attention; it had a sign in the window that said "Butterfly Cage." Well, of course, I had to see what a butterfly cage looked like. It was a circular tube maybe three feet long and 18 inches in diameter. They were there, three butterflies, just as pretty as you would expect. Well, maybe it was a little thing, but I was impressed. There were many such moments on the trip that involved things that left an impression—a human-sized Spiderman balloon draped across someone's window, a little plastic fisherman on a pier, the balcony of a house decorated with nets and buoys.

I was alone most of the trip, so the brief meetings I had when I came on the land tended to stick in my mind. That night, in Kingston,

Captain Tony is no fool. He's got inches to spare under the bridge.

I met a tugboat captain, Captain Tony. I showed him my card and told him what I was doing.

He told me he was delivering a tug into the shipyard for annual maintenance.

"Where is the tug?" I asked, assuming it must have been nearby.

"Coming up the river," he replied.

"But you're the captain?" I asked, surprised and a little confused. If he was there and he was the captain, why wasn't the tug there?

"It's because I am the captain," he explained.

"You lost me."

He explained that it was the first time the company had used the shipyard. There was some question of whether the tug could clear the bridge at Kingston.

"I'm going to film it clearing the bridge," he said, showing me the video cam he had with him.

"As captain, shouldn't you be steering the tug?" I asked.

"If that tug hits the bridge, I will be out of a job, but the mate is young, and he can get another job."

We continued talking, and Captain Tony had a lot of useful information that would help in my future travels. He told me what to look out for as I went up the river and how to stay away from the tugs and the props.

My evening accommodation was at Ms. Guessy's, which was not a B&B but just a room. But it was a very nice room on the fourth floor overlooking the waterfront stage. Yes, I said stage. I had the pleasure of being serenaded from my window by the Dixie Babes. These three ladies dressed in red mini-dresses and white ankle boots sang their hearts out to the Motown songs. But it was Sunday night, and the audience was only about 50 people.

Using my cell phone, I called home, where a party of 15 was gathered for an evening cookout. My friend placed the phone on a speaker for entertainment for the cookout. Live from Kingston, New York, to

The Dixie Babes

Virginia Beach, Virginia, the music was broadcast to the cookout group. Thank you, Dixie Babes—you passed on more joy than you know.

The next day, I continued up the Hudson to Troy. Coming from the south, I kept hitting the spring weather as I went north. The flowers and greenery on the Hudson were beautiful. Spring just kept happening as I continued north to connect to the Erie Canal.

The days and nights were taking on a normal routine, which was what I wanted. During the day, I concentrated on covering 50 to 65 miles at a clip before I had to refuel. I usually made two stops before final port at the end of the day. Depending on the winds, I could travel between 50 and 100 miles per day. That might not sound like a lot, but it was the spring weather, and it was windy. The wind was an issue from morning until night. Wind to a jet ski was anything greater than 10 miles per hour. The wind, unless blowing offshore, created waves of two feet, which in turn meant moment-by-moment challenges. I concentrated totally on the water and moving from one marker to the next.

Later, as the weather changed and I left the East Coast, I would cover more distance per day.

I always tried to get to the night port by 2 or 3 p.m. each day. This gave me time to refuel and deal with my special needs as a Bumblebee runner. Finding a cleat to tie the Bumblebee was not an issue, but unpacking the Bumblebee and getting to a motel often required some innovation. Normally I would get a small meal from the bar, but that was often where all the single traveling salespeople ate. Back in the motel room, there was review time, making notes on what was working and what needed to be replaced. I always looked over the next day's route, creating an "A" and a "B" port and picking fuel marinas on the way.

Then I listened to the VHF marine forecast and got my wireless e-mails and sent out e-mails. "Wher's lArRy NOW!!!" Before I had sent out my first two e-mails, the requests starting coming in from people wanting to be added to my e-mail list. Many were quite humorous. The e-mail list was growing. People were joining from all around the country. But if someone e-mailed, I replied. Sometimes that required a lot of tapping. Later, I would write the highlights of the day in my journal.

Some nights, I checked in to find out the odds for or against the trip with gambler Jim. Usually I tried to ignore it. But now and then, curiosity got the best of me, and I had to find out. Odds were staying the same. I thought that was odd. I had covered a lot of ground over the past few days. Odds should drop. Jim was still convinced, "He'll never make it."

Last I always called home twice. The first call was to my wife's cell phone just to advise her I was at such and such port. Later at 9:00 each evening, I called her to catch up on the day. I never told her any negatives; that would only heighten her concern and give her firepower to tell me to quit. But I had never quit before, and I was not going to then. My daily calls to her gave me a sense of security. If I did not make the first port call, she would know something had gone awry. She knew where I had last been and where I was headed. If I did not pop up, the troops would be called out to find the missing wave rider.

By the time my chores were done, I was tired and ready to go to sleep. I knew the next morning I could expect the unexpected.

Troy, New York, was the stepping-off point to the Erie Canal. The canal would be 340.7 miles east to west all the way across New York State. Troy was just above Albany, a small city trying to make a comeback, and, in time, it will. But the empty stores gave it a rundown quality. I stayed at a motel close to the small marina that had a long dock on the Hudson River. I accidentally dropped my glasses into the water there and watched them sink to the bottom. It was one of five pairs of I would lose on the trip.

In Troy, I prepared for the trip on the canal. I updated some goods and acquired some new items, including a water-resistant coat, rubber gloves, and heavy clothesline. The gloves and line were for the water locks. I had read that the locks had a lot of algae growth inside, which could make things quite nasty. The coat was the best find—bright red and lined with zippers and only 15 bucks. I would need it as I headed north. The Weather Channel showed nothing but cold fronts coming down from Canada.

The Erie Canal had some great history, and I would learn a lot about it over the coming days—the mules that pulled the boats through the locks originally and how the opening of the Erie had been the impetus behind much of the financial success of New York City. It wasn't used for commercial trade anymore; those days had passed. It was mostly used by pleasure boaters to traverse between the Great Lakes and the East Coast or by the locals.

June 4 and I was going to take on my first lock on the Erie Canal. I was up bright and early and was on the water by 7 a.m. The previous day, I had talked to a fellow boater on a 90-foot Hatteras. (Yes, I was a fellow boater, even if my vehicle was only 11 feet long. That was the beauty of boaters—they welcomed everyone on the water and would chat and exchange stories about where they had been and where they were going.) The 90-footer told me to be at the boat at 7 a.m., and I could tag along with them into the first lock. So there I was, right on the stern, when the 90-footer took off for the lock.

This was the first of 34 locks on the Erie Canal. Each lock took about 30 minutes to cycle, which could vary depending on how many boaters were going east or west. Locks were a simple process. Boats went from sea level to about 500 feet above sea level at the other end of the canal. Each lock was a step up. The boat came into the container at current sea level. The doors shut, and the container filled with water, which raised the water level 40 feet or so. Then the doors on the other side opened up, and the boat was 40 feet higher and ready to move onto the next lock, or the next step upward.

When we approached the lock, it looked like a container ship that had been cut open. I followed the 90-footer into it. The doors to the lock closed behind us. The walls were solid cement on both sides. An imposing chamber of gray steel and gray concrete, it was about 30 feet wide and 100 feet long. The enormous gray metal steel doors were about 60 feet high. I felt like a small piece of plastic in the water when I looked

The first Erie Canal lock

up at those doors slowly closing behind us. When the doors closed, the boom echoed through the chamber. The metal doors in front were closed. On top of the doors there was a small landing for the workmen to cross. A man crossing up there looked tiny from below.

Then the alarm went off to indicate that the lockmaster was operating the lock. He was warning anybody within 50 yards of the lock doors to stay away because of water turbulence. As the doors shut behind the 90-footer and me, I hung onto the rope and pushed the jet ski away from the walls.

I was so excited I called my friend Mr. Tim in Chicago. After all, I was getting closer to Chicago, where he lived.

"Guess where I am? My first lock on the Erie."

"Do you know what time it is?" he asked, half awake.

Oops. I forgot it was only 6:30 a.m. in Chicago.

"Go back to sleep. Sorry."

"Call me in two hours, Larry,"

The water began to flood in from underneath. I and the jet ski started to go up quickly. It was a 40-foot rise. With my whole body on the jet ski, I turned sideways to face the chamber wall and put out a foot so the jet ski didn't bump the wall.

The lock doors opened, and we sailed out, 40 feet higher.

After that first lock, I more or less had it down, though I never lost my awe of the locks on the canal. The locks could lift or lower you from 40 feet to six feet, depending on the lock and where it was on the canal. Often the locks were by small dams from the inflowing streams. But I quickly learned the routine to deal with the locks. I used my VHF marine radio to call the lockmaster and request entrance to the lock. I would inform him of my type of boat (at first there was surprise; later they knew I was coming) and tell him which direction I was going. "Lock 17," I would say, "this is the jet ski approaching from the east, heading west." The lockmaster would respond with the status of the lock and instructions.

When I entered the chamber, I would decide which wall I was going to stand by. I tried to stay back from the doors at the higher end of the canal because when they opened at the end of the process, there was some turbulence. Most locks had steel ladders in the wall of the chamber. Some boaters "walked" up the ladders with their hands or the boat hook as the chamber filled.

Each chamber was different, and I paid attention when entering. Where were the drop lines? What were the walls like? I would turn off the jet ski after I had positioned by the wall. Jet skis and boats had to shut off their motors because of the fumes. My rubber gloves intact and clothesline in hand, I would pull into the lock, attach to a ladder or hold a line, and up I would go. I kept the Bumblebee from hitting the walls of the lock by pushing off with my feet. The boaters had to maintain rubber bumpers off the bow and the stern of the boat plus keep a line on the hooks on the wall to hold the boat in place against the wall as the water level increased.

I would wait a safe time before I exited the lock after the gates were opened. There was often a surge then. Then I would push off from the wall and move back out into the canal.

I passed through eight locks my first day. Each lock and each lockmaster was great. The lockmasters on the Erie Canal were some of the best people I'd ever met. I even asked one of them, "Do they send you guys to customer service schools?" They were courteous and friendly and responsible, and I couldn't praise them enough. As I went through, they would ask me whether I was headed to the next lock, and then they would call ahead for me. They were looking out for me, and I appreciated it. Those guys were great!

The Erie Canal was generally narrow and shallow, probably not more than 12 feet deep. It was mostly a calm ride, little current. The wind was not a factor, so the water was glassy and slick. It was like taking a drive on a country road on a Sunday when there wasn't much traffic. I must admit that keeping it to 10 knots per hour was difficult. The first day, it was cloudy and cool (55 degrees), and by the end of the day, drizzle had set in. There was a lock about every 15 miles. Each lock was unique; each lockmaster was also unique and always friendly. There was no commercial traffic on the Erie Canal those days; they only serviced recreational vehicles.

By car you could see a lot of America, but you normally went from point to point, with very few stops in between. With the Bumblebee, I could travel at almost any speed and stop when I wanted to. But from the water, you saw the backside of cities and homes, and it was totally different from the usual view. It was a private view seen by only a few. It was very different from the scripted view presented by traveling the highways.

Gossip seemed to travel quickly along the Erie Canal. I guessed that between the boaters passing stories via VHF and the marinas and the lockmasters, word of the jet ski from Virginia traveled before me. The lockmasters seemed to know I was coming.

At lock 8, I called it a day. It was an interesting day but a long one. I hitched a ride with the lockmaster to the local motel, the old L&W Motel. It was a one-story motel built in a circle with 15 rooms, built about 1940. In the circle, there was a picnic table that had splinters the size of toothpicks. The ceiling of the room had glitter, and there wasn't much to provide nourishment but a Coke machine.

The motel owner didn't speak English, and it took some sign language before he realized that English was the only language I spoke. I ordered out some Chinese: $10 worth of chicken chow mein (minimum order), and that's a lot of chow mein. I shared it with five dogs that roamed the grounds around my favorite picnic table. Then I decided to call and let my wife know I had landed safely. The cell phone lit up but couldn't find a signal. I got out the phone card, but all the lines were busy on the phone card. It took three hours to get a phone call out. I felt like I was just the other side of nowhere.

The next morning, June 5, I walked out of the motel and thumbed a ride with a lockmaster who was going to work. I rode all day past lock

22 to Sylvan Beach at Skinners Marina. I was running hard that day because it was beginning to rain. After I went through one lock, the lockmaster said he would call ahead to the next lock so the lockmaster would have the doors open for me. I blasted out, hitting 55 all the way. Normally the trip would have taken 30 to 40 minutes. I was at the next lock in 10 minutes. He had the lock open. It was dark and cloudy, and the rain was heavier. "You sure did get here mighty quick for going 10 miles per hour," the lockmaster said and then added, "I'm going to turn my cheek on that offense." Then he gave me a real helping hand: "I want you to get to the motel, so don't even tie off. Keep the engine going, and stay in the middle of the lock. We're going to do this operation fast so you can get down the road."

I was glad to pull in soon after. I was 134 miles into the Erie Canal. As was the norm on this trip, the people at Skinners Marina couldn't have been more accommodating. Liz, the manager and daughter of the owner, gave me a ride to the local motel called Cinderella's. It was a very small and quaint city of maybe 5,000. The people in middle New York were as good natured as anybody you could meet anywhere. Dinner was roast beef and cost $11.50, all ya can eat, a home run compared to the five dogs and chicken chow mein of the night before. I walked around the city that night, which took maybe 15 minutes. It had a little amusement park and a small outdoor park. I could see the cities were changing compared to East Coast cities.

On June 6, the next day, Liz picked me up promptly at 8 a.m. and took me down to the marina and the jet ski. I started out slow; the muscles in my shoulders were hurting. Bengay helped.

That day my route took me across Lake Oneida, which was about 20 miles long and maybe three miles wide. Lake Oneida was shallow, and I knew that the wind could kick up there. Crossing it might be problematic.

Before I left the marina, a sailboater I was talking to felt sorry for me as I tried to dry out the gunnels, which were the right and left side of the Bumblebee where I placed my feet. He donated a genuine sponge so I could remove the cold water where my feet would be. To this day, I still have that sponge; it was another item I would never have put on my list originally.

Gossip traveled along the Erie Canal. The boaters passed stories via the VHF, and information and/or speculation passed from one boater to another at the marinas and the locks. The lockmasters also kept the traveler informed. I had heard the previous day that locks 23 and 24 were closed because of floodwaters. I wasn't sure whether it was rumor or fact. But that day the word was that the locks were still closed and boaters were backing up on the west side of Lake Oneida.

After crossing Lake Oneida, I went over to the west side and stopped at the local marina. There I was told that the locks were then open. By then, I wasn't sure exactly what was going on. But there was only one way to find out—go forward.

I came up to lock 23 and stopped. Lock 23 was probably the most heavily trafficked lock on the canal. I was told by the lockmaster that I could go through the lock only if I signed a waiver of damage. Markers were out of place, and the banks of the canal were flooded. There was floating debris in the canal. "There's going to be logs floating," the lockmaster said. "You might not be able to see where the canal is and go over the embankment. But just stay in the open areas, and you should be OK." However, they could not be held responsible, and I couldn't go through without signing the waiver.

What was I signing away? How bad was the flooding ahead of me? I would be the first boat to go through in two weeks. My shoulders ached, and the weather had been nasty—rainy and cold. I felt chilled and tired. I felt like I couldn't go back, and, unless I signed the waiver, I couldn't go forward. And there was still a lot of trip in front of me—thousands of miles.

But as I stood there reading the waiver, I thought back over all the wonderful people I had met and all the beautiful country I had seen. More of both would follow, I was sure. I was also sure that I wanted to complete the trip. I still had that desire. If anything, it had been rekindled the night before when my wife innocently asked, "Have you had enough?" I'm sure she didn't mean to, but it was exactly the wrong thing to say. It made me determined to continue. That and the gambling pool back in Virginia Beach.

You couldn't go backward in life. You had to go forward.

I signed the waiver and moved out into what looked like a flooded field, but I could make out the canal. I had the canal to myself from locks 23 to 27. I did clean out the carburetors but only where I would not disturb any boaters or property owners. I was told about midway through the canal that the 10-knot rule would not pertain to me as long as I was not jumping boat wakes or creating problems for other boaters.

At lock 25, the lockmaster wanted to give me a dollar to "run, Forrest, run." I thanked him but declined the offer.

"If everyone gave you a dollar, your trip would be paid for," he said.

That sincere and honest man was another wonderful lockmaster on the Erie Canal. Word was passing between the lockmasters that I was coming or had just passed through. I often heard the lockmaster hail me with, "run, Forrest, run."

Charlie was the lockmaster who ran lock 27. We chatted for a while before I entered the lock. Charlie had met John Moffett two years before. Moffett was on his second Bumblebee when Charlie saw him. Charlie didn't know what had happened to the first one. I felt invigorated again, knowing Moffett had been there before me. (Hmm, second Bumblebee.)

Meanwhile, I was still traveling with the actual GPS in my lap or hand. I had held it all the way from the eastern coast of New Jersey. Needless to say, I was tired of holding it. (Right then I didn't need it for directions, just to keep track of the miles.) I had called Halflooper about the mount for the GPS. He had said it had to come from the factory. So two days before, I had called the factory, and they had sent it to Miller's Marina. Then I called Miller's Marina to advise them that the part was coming.

Miller's Marina run by Steve Miller

That day I was approaching Miller's Marina on the canal. It was quite a sight. I had never seen a marina in such disrepair. The dock was two sticks and four planks and not exactly what I would call sturdy. But Steve, the owner, was there, and, sure enough, he had the GPS mount. Steve had a good sense of humor, and we shared several laughs. I explained my trip to Steve, and he informed me that the famous John Moffett had also stopped at his marina. Steve posed for a picture. A picture is worth a thousand words.

As I got on the jet ski and moved into the sunset, Steve waved and said, "Tell everyone about Miller's Marina. Run by Steve Miller! Like the band!"

I stopped that evening in Newark, New York. The motel was nice, but the bar was like the inside of a cave, with stalagmites growing from the ceiling.

I was really putting the miles behind me. The adventure had begun to take shape and meaning, and the business card was beginning to shock people. I had come a long way from Virginia, and the trip was now more than a dream. It was a living reality.

On June 7, the next day, I left Newark, New York, in full sunshine. I had not seen the sun in 10 days. I took off my coat and rode with my T-shirt on. It was a glorious spring day. The canal was smooth, the sky was blue, and the air was crisp but warm. Along the canal, trees were putting off white powder puffs that floated through the air and across the canal. It was like snow floating through the fresh air and into the water. Each puff drifted gracefully and languorously on the gentle breeze and then settled into the blue water. They floated around me and made the day a white dream. For a few minutes, I got lost in that dream.

A new feature of the canal was the low bridges, which were about 50 feet long and level with the street. This allowed about three feet from the top of the water to the bottom of the bridge. The height of the Bumblebee was 29 inches, which left about seven inches to get under the bridge. Before I went under the first bridge, I watched the water to be sure there were no ripples and that it was smooth. I didn't want to bang the Bumblebee or myself on the bottom of the bridge. Ducking as low as I could, I slowly took the Bumblebee under the bridge.

I just squeaked under this bridge by mere inches

My port that day was Brockport, New York. That was where I met the Great Bridge Master, George. Truly one nice guy, George got me free dockage, a motel room, a ride to the motel, and a tour of the bridge controls. George, if you read this, thanks for all your kindness. That was a wonderful day and a day that I needed. One great spirit lifter.

I left Brockport the next morning, heading for Tonawanda, New York. The western part of the Erie was just picture perfect. Spring was in the air, and the landscape was truly magnificent. Walking and biking trails lined the canal. There were also several parks off the canal.

I came down the canal, and there were some kids swimming off on the side of the canal. It was like the cover of some old *Post* or *Life* magazine from a forgotten America. But it was still there—the kids splashed and screamed with laughter as they jumped off the swing they had hooked to the bottom of the bridge.

I had a lot more bridges to scoot under, and at one point, I literally walked myself and the jet ski under the bridge.

The last two locks were the biggest, locks 34 and 35. I followed a yacht into the first lock. I was on his stern. The captain was on the stern holding his yacht in place as the lock began to fill. We began to talk. He was coming from Florida, headed for Michigan. He looked at my Bumblebee and said, "You know, they make water trailers for those jet skis. I saw one in Annapolis." Sure enough, he had seen the one I gave to Tim, the dock boy. It was a small world. What a hoot! We both laughed when I explained the coincidence. But it wasn't really a coincidence. Boaters traveled the same routes but at different times. We all shared the same neighborhood and met the same neighbors.

As we came out of lock 34, we went right into lock 35. On the chart, they looked like they were a mile apart, so the quick transition was a surprise.

As I came by one of the parks by the canal, I saw a group of people on the green lawn. A young woman in a white wedding gown was walking under a large old tree that grew by the canal. I thought it might be an outdoor wedding, so I decided to stop and watch. I soon realized that it was the wedding rehearsal. "Hey, you're missing a groom," I said.

They signaled for me to join them, and before I realized it, I was playing the part of the groom, wet suit and all. We walked down the sidewalk together, me in my wet suit and she in her glorious white gown, with white veil, and holding white flowers. They invited me to the wedding. She e-mailed me two months later that all went well with the wedding.

I had traveled 492 miles from Troy, New York, to Tonawanda, New York. I said farewell to the great Erie Canal.

Then it was onto new waters of the Niagara River just below Niagara Falls.

The Holiday Inn on Grand Island provided the first vacation I'd had since the start of the trip. I prepared for the rest of the trip. It was Sunday. I dried out all my contents from the Bumblebee and washed clothes. Next I had to get to the local West Marine. As luck would have it, there was a West Marine right on the water about five miles south of me in Buffalo. Sunday on the Niagara River in the early part

A good substitute for the groom

of late spring was busy. The boaters were out in force. The winter was over in this hard northern country, and the locals were out to enjoy the water.

On my way over to the West Marine, a water patrol eyed my Bumblebee. He passed me and circled for a closer look and then requested that I stop.

"Are you over 21?" he asked.

"Well, duh, look at the gray hair."

He looked sheepish but immediately jumped to the next question. "Do you have the following safety equipment?"

I pointed out how well equipped I was, and, yes, I had all that was required.

"Do you have New York insurance?" he asked out of frustration.

"I have insurance that covers America," I said, looking at him like he had four ears.

I wasn't sure what he wanted. I think he was just venting because Bumblebees as a group presented problems for the boating public. I had to admit there were a lot of abuses within the sport group, but I had also been a boater, and I had seen many more violations from the boaters than from the Bumblebees.

Part of Sunday chores included running down my charts for the upcoming crossing of the Great Lakes. The charts I had went through the Erie Canal up to Buffalo. Because there were so many charts involved in the Great Loop and I had limited space on the Bumblebee, I had broken the charts down into groups for various parts of the trip. The charts and books were discarded along the route as I passed the areas. At some points, I even did this page by page. Why dry a whole book when you needed only the remaining 100 pages out of 300? I needed a new set of charts for the trip from Buffalo to Chicago.

My mother was part of the of the three-member ground support team. The other members of the land crew were all named Tim—Mr.

Tim from Chicago, Illinois, who was handling the Web site and Mr. Tim out of Fort Myers Beach, Florida, who was arranging some future necessities. If you meet a Tim, he's a champ among men.

Mom was in charge of handling the charts. I called her at least twice a week and gave her an update on my location. She took a magic marker and marked off the map as I traveled it. Mother, like most senior citizens, had her fixed schedule of doctor's appointments, shopping, and restaurants. Any abrupt change in her schedule created chaos. I had to call her two days in advance to tell her where to send the next set of charts. I'd given her the name and address of a motel, so off I went to pick up the charts. Yes, the charts were there. Hip Bee Mom was on the job.

The rest of Sunday was a day of relaxation and pleasure at the marina. Sparkling clear water lapped the docks. The marina was full of people. Out of practice from winter, boaters tried to dock their boats at the marina. Docking a boat might look easy, but it wasn't. You had to maneuver the boat into the boat slip with 12 inches on each side while fighting the wind and current and trying to focus, with people shouting ("Left! Right! Stop!"). Let's not forget that you couldn't see the dock, and there wasn't any brake like a car. Everybody got a little anxious, especially the boat owner in the next slip. Those near the boat trying to dock pitched in and helped. The enthusiasm was always there with each boat docking or, should I say, boat slamming.

Most of these boaters had 25-footers, but, again, they did not travel more than five or 10 miles in any direction. Most of the boaters couldn't figure out what my story was. I had a dark tan by then (much darker than the normal summer tan) and Virginia registration plates, and I didn't fit in. When I said I was going to navigate Lake Erie on a jet ski, the reaction was astonishment. People approached me for my story, and I gave them my card and told them where I had been and where I was going. Word traveled very quickly through the marina. There were lots of questions such as: "How do you get fuel? What made you do this? Aren't you scared? Where are you going next? Do you have family? Will you be in Guinness's World Records? What made you do this?"

There were so many questions that sometimes I wasn't fast enough to give a good or any answer, so I gave them my business card. That seemed to satisfy most of them and answer their questions. I was glad I'd had those cards printed and spent all that time drying them out that day early on in the trip. There were many marinas with many people who had many questions. The cards saved a lot of wear and tear on my vocal chords.

The Bumblebee was serviced the following Monday. The dealership also had all-terrain vehicles (ATVs) for sale. As I looked at those ATVs, I realized that some of the concepts could be transferred to a Bumblebee. The one thing that caught my eye was an optional item for the ATV—a carrying trunk. The trunk mounted right on the back of the ATV with a carrying rack and a great lid with hinges and locks. It looked like it had potential for me. I picked it up from the ATV and

Happiness is a luggage compartment

marched it back to the service center where my Bumblebee was being worked on. It fit on the back of the Bumblebee perfectly and even wrapped around the seat. It was a dream come true, and, damn, look at the space that trunk had on the inside. The service people looked at me as if I had five eyes. If they had traveled with the carpetbagger bags and had the daily routine of trying to dry my damp and soaked belongings, they would have understood.

"OK, guys," I said, "let's mount it and mount it permanently. It has to withstand all that Mother Nature can throw at me."

The mechanics worked until dusk, and it was minutes from darkness when I was put back in the water. I had a 10-minute run back to Grand Island across the Niagara River, the same river where the water patrol had previously stopped me. The Bumblebee had no running lights, so I went full steam across the river. We made it.

Before I walked away from the jet ski for the night, I did one more take of the new prize luggage compartment. The next day I could finally load it up and get rid of those Clampet bags. There's happiness! "It's the small things" was never truer.

That night I answered my e-mail:

```
Subject: Where'sLarry NOW

From: <waverider4222@palm.com>

Date: Sun, 9 Jun 2002 14:24:08 +0000 (GMT)

To: <all@all.com>

Well just 5 miles north of Buffalo NY,,yep,,,up
next to Niagara Falls,the Errie Canal was great
all 35 locks and 10 bridges which I could squize
under (some with less than 4 inches),,,If you
could see the jet ski I look like Jed Clampett
from the Beverly Hillbillies, with my bags
bungee to the ski,,,the lock master looked out
for me by calling ahead to each station telling
them when I would be coming through,,,they would
say "GO FORREST GO",,,great people,,,the western
```

```
Errie Canal is a post card picture,,,will stay
here at Grand Island Holiday Inn for a few
days,,need rest and relaxtion,,,who would think
you need R & R from jet sking (go figure),,
```

By then I had traveled 1,150 miles, or about one-fifth of the trip. I had more than 4,450 miles to go. Each part of the trip had its personality. This one was as friendly and warm as the people in upstate New York. The weather hadn't been that good—cold and raining too much of the time. But the people were delightful, and the Erie Canal was a wonder.

I had put some serious miles under the jet ski by then. Every mile added a little bit more to my self-confidence. Jim should have lowered his odds. But I heard he was keeping the same odds. Mom wanted the long odds: more money for her because she had no doubt I'd make it all the way. I wondered whether I could anonymously get into the game. By then I had the self-confidence to put down some hard cash.

Chapter 5
Tests:
The Eerie Lake Erie

The next morning (June 11) I happily packed my new trunk on the jet ski. Room to spare! I did a merry little "yes!" dance on the pier and high-fived myself. The sun was out, and I was a happy camper. Off for Lake Erie!

Then I headed out into the Black Lock Channel. Destination Black Rock Lock, which had a delightful, ominous ring. The channel could take commercial vessels up to 625 feet long with drafts of 21 feet. Needless to say, at 11 feet long and 30 inches high, I wasn't quite in that category. The upper end of the Black Rock Lock was at Lake Erie level; the lower end reentered the Niagara River (where I was). The water came in from Lake Erie to go downstream to the Niagara. The lock chamber was a long, narrow construction—650 feet long and 70 feet wide, with 100-foot-high walls when the guard gates were closed. The lift there was about five feet.

I approached it slowly. The lockmaster was all-powerful. He could let you pass or not. His word was law. No higher appeal. Each approach to the lock was filled with some anxiety: would he let me pass? Would all go well in the lock? How would this lockmaster react to the jet ski? Would it pass the reality test with him or just be more flotsam? The red signal light located at the end of the dock told me to wait. There I came upon a fellow boater, also waiting for the lock. After a few hellos and "Where you going?" he said that of course I could go into the lock with him.

But as I entered the lock with his boat, the lockmaster spotted me.

"Hey," he yelled, "I cannot allow you to enter."

I smiled as pleasantly as I could and explained my mission: "I'm doing the Great American Loop. You know, around the—"

"You can't go in, guy!"

I didn't want it to turn into a "bad day at Black Rock."

"I've already passed through 35 locks and no problem," I explained.

"I've got no guidelines for a jet ski," he said.

We went back and forth with more exchanges. I pleaded and explained. It was a difficult negotiation. Finally, he relented. I sighed with relief as he directed me beside the other boat to the west wall. I didn't blame him. He was just doing his job. I cut the engine. The water gushed in, and the chamber filled.

Transitioning from one stage to another, protected yet vulnerable, the locks had a ritualistic quality. In a sense, each lock was another small birth because with each lock, I gained just a little more self-confidence, and with each lock, I was more firmly committed to my new adventure. Each time the gate opened and I passed out of the chamber, there was a slight feeling of relief and jubilation. A new "something" would then begin. And it always did.

Inside the Black Rock Lock (which I felt deserved its own rap song), I talked with the new boater friend I had just met. He was finishing his run into Michigan, but he wasn't sure about the waves on Lake Erie. Because I would be entering the opening to Lake Erie at least 15 minutes before he would, we agreed that I would radio back to him and advise about the conditions. The lock gates opened again, and out we went.

Fifteen minutes later, I hit Lake Erie. Then I knew where the "eerie" came from. It was not a lake but an ocean. Water devoured the horizon. There was nothing on the horizon but choppy waves. It was overcast and foreboding. The wind was kicking up three- to four-foot waves. It was going to be rough.

I radioed back and reported the conditions to my fellow boater. "I think I'll sit it out," he said.

I considered the situation. Big waves and one hell of a big lake. My port of call was Dunkirk, New York. The run across that part of Lake Erie was about 48 miles. Could I do it? I'd never been on that water before, and it was a stormy day. But I had been on the Chesapeake Bay in a nor'easter. Could it be that bad? Surely it couldn't be worse. I felt I could handle it and decided to go for it.

Would I have done it at the beginning of the trip? Probably not. But I had spent a lot of days on the water. I had some serious miles under the jet ski.

Out I went into Lake Erie. The jet ski moved out quickly. The first 10 miles were hard, but the waves were more like ocean swells, with a slow rise and fall. It was the last 38 miles—they were a kicker all the way. These were the most challenging winds and waves of the trip. The waves peaked up to five feet high, and I went up with them, the jet ski at a right angle to the sky. Then another wave hit, six feet high, coming in fast behind the first. Then another, following fast again. It was a quick and hard bombardment of wave after wave. My hands gripped the throttle. The new GPS mount was holding. The gloves my mother had sent with the last shipment of charts kept my hands warm. The jet ski roared up against the next wave. The water slapped into my face and eyes. But at least the water was fresh, not saltwater, so it didn't sting my eyes. Luckily, I was facing the waves. I could see what was coming at me and be ready for it.

I quickly learned that a west wind on Lake Erie was an easy match for a nor'easter on the Chesapeake. Lake Erie was a shallow lake, and the wind could kick up some real devils there. Each wave drenching was a cold shock over my body. The waves kept coming. I was thankful that by then I had dropped 20 pounds, and my hands were like vice gripes. My body couldn't have taken the beating at the beginning of the trip. Just when I thought the worst was over, another wave hit. I kept my focus. Lake Erie raged. I had one object. Get to land. Get to Dunkirk.

Finally I saw the marina at Dunkirk. Relief. As I came into the marina, I was determined I wouldn't face another day like that. Why had I been so foolish to attempt it? Taking off in bad weather on a lake I did not know. Though a part of me knew I wouldn't do it again, another part of me was glad I had.

All those bright days, my lungs full of air and flying over strange waters in somewhat strange lands had begun to change me in ways I couldn't quite articulate and still can't. There's something wild in everyone's blood. There's something that wants freedom and air and a one-to-one contest with Mother Nature. I'd met Lake Erie when she was mad. She landed a series of quick and furious punches. But I'd taken what she had to dish out. We had our contest, and, though I wouldn't say that I won, I had walked away whole.

As I came into the harbor, the blood was pumping full force. My heart was still throbbing hard in my chest. The colors seemed more intense. The air, though cold, felt invigorating. I would remember that day.

Jim wasn't collecting on his bets yet.

The trunk had withstood the beating on the waves. So at least the afternoon packing and unpacking was so much easier. In the motel room, I took off the wet suit boots. My toes immediately felt like they had shriveled up. My toenails felt too long for my toes. Slowly I began to warm up. My body had taken a beating out there, and it was setting in.

The following day (June 12) I woke up to chilled winds out of the west 10 to 25 miles per hour. The sky was overcast. Lake Erie was having another bad-tempered day. No, I was not going out to meet her that day. And despite my previous day's victory, that day I was feeling beat up and sad. It was, I think now, the inevitable collapse and exhaustion that came after a huge exertion or challenge met. The sense of coming down from an unwanted but exhilarating high was hitting me. The gray clouds made me feel homesick. And in those cold waters, I'd forgotten all about wanting to see a manatee.

Dunkirk was a pretty rural town. I went down to the marina and worked on the Bumblebee. A guy walked up to me.

"Nasty weather," I said.

"Yep, it sure is," he said and then paused. "You're not from around here."

"Virginia Beach."

"Hey, I got a time-share unit in Virginia Beach."

I smiled. I felt the taste of home. He was an electrician working on the electrical pedestal. We proceeded to strike up a conversation about restaurants and bars in both my home, Virginia Beach, and there in Dunkirk, his home.

After he left, I moseyed around the marina for a while. The electrician had helped me get out of the funk I was in, but I still felt restless and lost. Talking about home had been reassuring, but it also made me miss it more.

I spotted a 52-foot Bluewater in a dry dock.

"Nice boat," I said to the guy standing on it.

"Thanks," he smiled.

We introduced ourselves. The owner was Jeff, and he had been in port for about 10 days. Jeff was doing the Great Loop also, but he had hit something in the water and bent his shafts and props. Jeff was from California and was about 60 years old. His dream was to run the Great Loop.

His dream was the same as mine. He was doing it on a 52-footer, and I was doing it on an 11-footer.

"Is the wife with you?" I asked, making conversation with this newfound soul mate.

He laughed. "She hates boating."

"Mine, too," I laughed.

"She told me to go chase my dream, and if it doesn't work out, come home."

"Mine, too."

We laughed together. I'd found my twin. We exchanged a few stories of the Great Loop. Finally, I wished him well and said that I hoped we would cross paths again.

I was feeling better by then. Those two strangers had changed my whole mood. Over the trip, that was almost always true. About the moment I got blue and fainthearted, some stranger would come along, and we'd share something. And almost instantly my mood would change again.

That night I got a call from a friend who said Jim hadn't changed the odds on the bet. He was still certain I'd never make it, despite the fact that I was on Lake Erie. My friend said he thought more were betting on me than against me. I told him to keep an eye on Jim that he didn't skip out of town without paying people because he was going to owe some big bucks.

The next day (June 13) I was rested and ready go to again. I took off for Erie, Pennsylvania. The wind had shifted in the morning to come out of the north-northeast at five to 10 miles per hour. It was cloudy, and the temperature was between 60 and 70 degrees. They predicted it would stay like that for a few more days. Where was summer? There the coast had a small beach with cliffs beyond. Unlike my first encounter with Lake Erie, that day was relatively painless. The lake was far better humored and gave me a pleasant run.

Erie, Pennsylvania, was a very nice city. The symbol for Erie was the fish. A fish statue or plastic mold was everywhere, humanized, symbolically displaced from the waters and into the streets. At more than six feet high and very plump, the fish looked like cartoons. Appropriately named "Sexy Sadie," one fish was green with big pink lips and wide eyes and was caught in a merry twist. I gave it a friendly kiss of a greeting.

There was a black fish with purple lips, caught in the same position of a fish leaping up in the air over the water. Then I encountered a blue and red fish on a pedestal. While Sexy Sadie remained my favorite, I gave each of the others a greeting of some sort, well, at

Sexy Sadie gets a kiss

least a pat on its smiling head. The cartoon-like fish gave the city a merry feeling.

I picked up my e-mail. “How’s your ass?” one asked. I replied, tapping in the letters one by one.

Subject: Where’s Larry NOW

From: <waverider4222@palm.com>

Date: Thu, 13 Jun 2002 21:05:06 +0000 (GMT)

To: <all@all.com >

In Erie PA today headed to Cleveland OH tomorrow,,,got stuck in Dunkirk NY for a day due to winds,,,dam the weather has not been to helpful (cloudy, 60-70’s) no summer here yet! I assume they get one,,,,Well I get lots of questions, but the main one is how is your ass and everything connected,,,TIP of the day "buy stock in Lotrimin, Preparation H, Bengay and Vaseline, I am buying it as a product and they all work" (lol),,,each day brings a totally new experience with new people ,cities (towns /villages/townships) and each one has a MAIN street,,,Lake Erie is a shallow lake anywhere from 5 to 20 feet so the wind creates havoc with me,,,I learned what 20 -25 mille an hour west wind was like,,,will not repeat that one,,, well thats all to report today (meeting lots of boaters doing the same trip),,,sometimes I can not respond to emails because my wireless system will not connect,,,it’s like your cell phone roaming but not getting the air waves at all,,,seems like I get good connection at the larger towns.

Larry

June 14, the next day, I woke up to good weather. The wind would be in my favor in the morning and would come out of the west in the afternoon. I left Erie for Ashtabula, Pennsylvania. I went 41 miles at 45 to 50 miles per hour and arrived in Ashtabula in 70 minutes. It was a great run, definitely the best I had had so far on Lake Erie.

Anyone who spent any time on the water knew there was a big difference between traveling on land and traveling on water. Of course, the land was living, but you didn't feel it so directly or dramatically, particularly not on a superhighway. These days you could barely take your eyes off the road, and a good deal of the time you spent looking at the back of someone else's vehicle.

The water was alive. It danced, it heaved, it sank, it swirled, it turned, and it flattened. It was exciting and threatening at the same time, a joy and a misery. It was moody and stabilizing. Even though these days it was partly controlled by dams, lanes, and permits, you could still find something wild out there. Long highway trips became more crowded and less and less appealing. On the highway I had to stay in a lane; on the water the Bumblebee could zip anywhere. On the rivers, bays, and lakes, something free returned. Out there on the water, something of your soul returned—wild, dreaming, full of the adventure and the encounter, and graced with the reflections that organized the dream. The melody was on the water. Life without being on those vast bodies of water was a song without a tune—in short, no song at all.

When I arrived in Ashtabula, it was still early, 8:20 a.m. The wind had not yet changed direction. A major west-to-east storm was now predicted to come down from Wisconsin, and I knew it would keep me landlocked for several days. Cleveland was another 71 miles.

I wanted to go on to Cleveland, and it was still so early in the day. But I also remembered that wild run to Dunkirk. I didn't want to repeat it.

I asked a local, "Do you think the weather will hold until I get to Cleveland?"

"Might, might not," he replied.

"Well, in your experience here, with this kind of weather front moving in, do you think I've got several more hours before it hits?"

"Might, might not," he replied.

"Well, thank you."

"But you don't want to be on the lake when the wind kicks in from the west."

"Well, thank you," I said.

I approached another local and basically repeated the same conversation.

I took a quarter out of my pocket and threw it up in the air and caught it. Heads I go; tails I stay. Heads.

As I left Ashtabula, the cliffs were lower, and the land was flatter than the first part of the trip that day. But there the waterfront had bulkheads, large chunks of concrete placed on the shore to block the waves.

Six miles out, the wind shifted to the west at 20 to 25 miles per hour. It was the ride to Dunkirk all over again. In addition, the bulkheads along the waterfronts created a backwash to Lake Erie. For every two feet forward, I felt like I was going one foot backward. I was moving ahead at 10 miles per hour. It was going to be a long 70 miles. Lake Erie was kicking again. The waves were again coming in at five to six feet high. The jet ski bobbed around like a cork on top of the water. It was a nightmare.

Glancing toward the shore, I spotted a police car on the land that was following me up the coast on the coastal highway. Someone must have called them to tell them a jet ski was having trouble on the water. At one point, they stopped and were waving at me, yelling for me to come in. I waved back and indicated no, I wasn't coming in. They kept shouting. I kept going, and soon they were back in the police car following me again.

I knew a bigger front was coming in. That meant it was Cleveland or nothing. I knew the best thing to do was just keep pushing forward. At worst, I thought, the Bumblebee would conk out, and I'd have to float to shore. That was my "worst-case scenario." Drowning wasn't on my agenda, or even considered as a possibility, though obviously it was.

So I pushed forward. But I didn't like seeing those cops tracking me from land. Did they really think I was in serious trouble? No way. Finally the cops gave up and disappeared.

I ate some water. It was in every orifice of my body. My eyes, my mouth, my ears were all flooded. I cursed the lake. "Not today," I yelled at her. She slapped back with another wave. "Not today!" I repeated. Another slap. Mean bitch of a lake.

I finally came into Cleveland, Ohio, via "the Flats," a developed area of restaurants and bars right off the water that had probably originally been an industrial area. I was glad to pull in. I had survived another round with Ms. Erie.

Subject: Where's Larry NOW

From: <waverider4222@palm.com>

Date: Sat, 15 Jun 2002 00:50:09 +0000 (GMT)

To: <all@all.com >

Get your road atlas out,,,Cleveland Ohio,,,yes moved 115 miles today from Erie to Cleveland,,,if you look at the weather channe you will see a big low pressure over Lake Erie,,,west winds 15 to 25 winds,,,which are BAD!,,,,, like a North Eastern on the Chesapeake Bay,,,3 to 4 foot waves,,not good for me a CORK in the water,,,so it looks like I will have to stay land locked for a few days, (no one told Lake Erie about summer). I knew the wind was going to get bad so I left Erie PA at 6:30 AM , first 45 five mile was wonderful (I traveled at 45 to 50 miles per hour),,,wind caught me on the last 65 miles,,,oh well,,,I guess I will take in the city,,,real clean downtown,,"Rock and Roll Hall of Fame" plus lots of culture things (I can use all the culture I can get),,,sidenote, my jet ski holds 18 glaaons of gas and I get 4.5 to 5 miles per gallon so in theory I can ride 80 to 90 miles (I would never test that theory),,,,well thats all the news,,last note, met my first

```
unfriendly people,,do not buy fuel for your boat
at Commodore's Club Marina, just my way of passing
the word about noncustomer marinas (lol) have a
good weekend

larry
```

The Downtown Holiday Inn Select in Cleveland was my home for the next few days. It was the first time that I had the opportunity to pull the Bumblebee out of the water and give it a total clean up and wax job. Because of bad weather, I had time on my hands to tweak waterproofing my stuff and pick up those items I had to give up in Annapolis. By the end of the first day, I had obtained all my backup items and some improvements. The only items I held back on were extra fuel tanks, a tent, and a sleeping bag. The fuel tanks had to be a special brand that would fit in the gunnels of the Bumblebee. Based on my informational books, it looked like obtaining fuel on Lake Erie would not be an issue, but I wasn't sure about Lake Huron. I had Halflooper express mail the fuel tanks from Virginia Beach to Mr. Brian, a friend who lived on Lake Huron in Michigan. The tent and sleeping bag could wait till I got to Chicago.

Given the weather conditions, I tried to calculate the average distance I could make each day. Because of the northern cold spring, it looked like 70 miles per day was the most possible on the Great Lakes, but that calculation was dependent on the height of the waves. At that point, I had completed 1,213 miles, or 23 percent of the Great Loop.

That night I went down to the Flats —a lot of restaurants, bars, and disco party places—very clean and safe. The streets were lined with two- or three-story brick buildings with inviting neon signs. The lights reflected off the nearby water. It was a party every night there.

As usual, I was sitting at a bar and was minding my own business when three couples came in and sat down.

Out of my side vision, I noticed one of the men eyeing me strangely. "How much golf you play?" he asked finally.

"Golf?"

"You got to play a hell of a lot of golf."

I smiled. He was referred to how dark my tan was. I was burnt brown from days on the water.

"It's not golf," I said and explained my adventure. Then they all had questions. Between the rapid-fire questions, the suspicious bartender, and the loud music, it was lively, to say the least.

The bartender doubted one of the young women was of age. He asked for her identification. I noticed she wasn't carrying a purse.

"No problem," she said.

I didn't see any pockets, so I was intrigued.

She reached under her T-shirt. The T-shirt was tight across an ample and inviting bosom. She gracefully extracted the driver's license from her bra.

"I hope he doesn't ask for your credit card," her friend quipped.

But I sort of hoped he would.

It was Sunday, June 16, a good day to relax. I was still in Cleveland. The wind was still kicking the lake around, so I walked around downtown Cleveland and visited the Rock and Roll Hall of Fame. It was a

Guitars at the Rock and Roll Hall of Fame in Cleveland, Ohio

modern pyramid-shaped glass building. The outside was decorated with that mainstay of rock and roll, the steel guitar. The 150 guitars each stood 10 or 12 feet and were painted all colors or combinations of colors.

The John Lennon exhibit was on. I had gone from big colorful fish to big colorful guitars in a few short days. While old cities still had all the grand monumental buildings, I also thought that these modern symbols brought a playful, childlike quality to the inner-city environment that I didn't remember from 30 years ago. But 30 years ago, rock and roll was new, and nobody would have ever dreamt of giving it a museum.

The next day was again bad. I mounted the American flag on "the Trunk." The Bumblebee was all shined up and looking good again. After those few days of rest, I also was whole again and looking good. But the weather still wasn't cooperating.

Standing on the dock, looking out, I resented this forced layover. Damn the weather and the Canadian soldiers. Cleveland had a bug nicknamed the Canadian soldier because it looked like a tin soldier with four legs. They didn't bite. They just landed on you, mated, and dared you to brush them off. There were swarms of them. I could see the black clouds of those insects over the water from the land. I would have to remember to keep my mouth shut out on the jet ski. Right then I slapped them around from circling my head. I was restless. Beginning to feel like grass was growing under my feet. Feeling the need for water.

The next day arrived (June 18), and finally it looked like a good day for the Bumblebee. The winds were coming out of the northeast at five to 10 miles per hour, with waves at one to two feet. I left Cleveland headed for: (A) Sandusky, Ohio, or (B) Put-in-Bay, Ohio. It felt good to be back on the water. Above Cleveland the shoreline was all rock with beautiful homes dotting the shore.

I came off Lake Erie into a rock canal that led to a city that was all on the water—Vermillion, Ohio. Canals ran through the city. Hats off to a great-looking city.

Then I was back out onto Lake Erie, where I came to Cedar Point Amusement Park—yep, it was a big one. It boasted more roller coasters than anywhere in the world, and it seemed not a vain boast. The yellow spirals of roller coaster whipped up into the air like heads of giant, mythic snakes. The coasters climbed straight up in the air and then whirled around lower to the ground. But I wasn't a thrill seeker (well, not with roller coasters). After taking a few pictures, I blasted off again on the jet ski.

Put-in-Bay (PIB) was one of three islands about 10 miles off the shore of Ohio with local ferry service. It was a heavy tourist spot. As I got closer to PIB, the boating traffic increased markedly. It was a town with two faces. By day, it was a family community, with kids in the park and wholesome families out and about. By night, it was Key West. In fact, the locals called it the Key West of the north. Tourists made their reservations well ahead of time because there were four motels on the island and they filled up fast. On the island, the mode of transportation was the golf cart. Thousands of carts traversed the byways, but the people were careful drivers by day and by night as well. I highly recommend PIB as a keeper.

In each city I visited, I always got a local newspaper. I'd find it on the street stands or in local stores. Then I'd take it with me to dinner or back to the motel and read through it, fascinated. Being from an area with two million people, I loved these hometown papers. Each was a snapshot of small-town life. At PIB, five students had just graduated from high school, pictures of graduates included, of course. The mayor of PIB had just resigned abruptly, shocking the community. The mayor had some sharp words with a local restaurant owner, which in turn caused the chief of police to resign. Then, tit for tat, the mayor himself resigned. It was a situation that I sensed was loaded with intrigue and drama, but I couldn't quite figure out why any of them resigned.

I wasn't prepared to be the talk of the town, but word got around. I spent the evening at the local pool bar, drinking my favorite beer, cooking my own hotdog, and getting my hair cut at the bar. PIB had the longest bar in the Unites States—I did not get the measurements, but it was a solid city block long. Life was good in PIB.

The next day, June 19, I left PIB with no definite port of destination. For the first time, I had no clear idea of where I would port that day. The wind was coming from the southeast at five to 15 with two- to three-foot waves. I knew that was manageable if I got out early before the winds really picked up. That day would put me in open waters; it was 33 miles across that part of the lake to the mouth of the Detroit River. Halfway across there was a small five-acre island. Otherwise, there was no land in sight. It would be the first time since Chesapeake Bay that I could not see the land. GPS don't fail me now.

As I quickly realized, using a GPS on a jet ski in that critical moment was not like using a GPS on a 40-foot yacht. A yacht could go on autopilot (like cruise control), but it also kept the same heading. And a yacht was steady enough to keep a reading with the GPS. A yacht could stay on a straight line out in the middle of the blue with no markers in sight. But when you were riding on a jet ski, the craft was bouncing all over the place, getting knocked about by the second. It was impossible to read the GPS and stay on a straight line based on it. And there was no land or water marker to fix the eye on. It wasn't like they had street signs out there.

But there were large white floating clouds in a crisp blue sky. I found the only way I could keep a straight line was to put my eye on a cloud that took my attention and mark my course toward the cloud. There was one obvious problem—the clouds moved. But I could usually get a fix for at least 10 minutes before I had to pick a new cloud. My eyes fixed on the top whirl of a large white cloud, but slowly the whirl was flattening.

My heartbeat was picking up. Lake Erie had decided to hand me another challenge—no more of the obvious punches for now. Now she was going to let me drift off into the blue horizon with no bearings and run out of gas out there with no one around. My breathing was shallower, and I gripped the throttle tighter. The usual smile on my face faded. I fixed my eye on another cloud that looked like a bird. I followed it until the bird became wisps. Time for another cloud. I cursed the lake under my breath. It wasn't fun being slapped around and possibly losing my bearings. It was beginning to seem like forever out there on Lake Erie, and for a while, I seriously thought I might be lost.

Finally I saw the small island in the middle of Lake Erie. It was topped with green, and gulls circled directly above it. Then I spotted two other boats. I had made it.

Should I land and catch my breath and my courage? I elected to go forward. After all, the Detroit River was only 18 miles northwest, and I would be seeing channel markers in about 12 miles. Piece of cake, I thought.

Twelve miles by car is a piece of cake; 12 miles with no land in sight on an 11-foot Bumblebee re-fried all the nerves. After I had vowed not to let Lake Erie get me again, there I was locked in another form of combat with her. But I had no choice. I had to push on.

After about 13 miles, I saw a channel marker. The marker bobbed in the water like a friendly hand waving me in. I felt like waving back. Then I saw some offshore fishing boats—I knew the fishermen had to be wondering who the crazy nut was. As usual, I waved. Their return waves had a stunned, uncertain quality. I could almost hear them saying, "What in the hell is he doing out there?"

Once inside the Detroit River, I felt secure. I knew I could again rely on my instruments for exact navigation. I was riding the river between Lake Erie and Lake Huron. It was a nice run, with Canadian flags on the right and U.S. flags on the left. By then I was aiming for Port Huron, the northernmost town before entering Lake Huron.

As I got closer to Lake Huron, I could feel the tide gaining strength. I reached the southern point where Lake Huron was feeding into the Detroit River. The current had to be running 15 to 20 knots. I decided to go into Port Huron for the day. I traveled past the city and into the suburban area, where I found the Bridgeport Yacht Club. They were very excited about having me join them for the night, and I very much appreciated it. It had been a long and anxious 124 miles.

Again, I found my local newspaper. It was honoring John Inngram McMorra. That day he was the oldest man in the United States. John was 113 years old. Congratulations, John!

I picked up my e-mail. Two more fans had joined the cyberspace vigil. That cheered me up. I decided to answer my e-mail while I could still tap the letters in.

```
Subject: Where's Larry NOW

From: <waverider4222@palm.com>

Date: Wed, 19 Jun 2002 22:16:37 +0000 (GMT)

To: <all@all.com >

I guess I need to go back to the last Travel
update which was in Cleveland OH,,,,yep left
there on tuesday,,,wind was on my side after
waiting 3 days,,,I was going to Sandusky /Cedar
Point Amuesment Park, but another boater sug-
gested I go to Put-In-Bay and he was 100% cor-
rect,,,,stopped at the Cedar Point Amuesmant
Park and took some pictures but they are known
for there roller coasters,,, moved on to Put-In-
Bay (PIB),,,it is an Island in Lake Erie,,,,,and
just like any other island it lives up to it's
reputation as a PARTY ISLAND,, today was a long
jet ski run 124 miles but I wanted to get off
Lake Erie,,now in Port Huron, southern tip of
MI,,,,,will be visiting a friend of mine in two
days "Brian Hagle",,,he claims he has federal
express in 2 cases of Miller Light just for me
(in bottles) seems like they only carry home
brew up here,,,,, so much for the Erie tales.

larry
```

June 20. That was the day I was going onto Lake Huron, a new body of water with all its unknown challenges. I was up early to prepare. I went to the dock to fuel the jet ski, but the yacht club didn't sell fuel.

They suggested a small marina across the river. Off I went. As I came up to the marina, I saw the big sign: "Party Marina." It consisted of four boat slips and two outdoor tables with umbrellas and eight chairs. One hell of a party, I thought, amused.

I tried to find the owner, but the marina was locked. But I did come across a guy who said he could start the pumps so I could fuel, and then he went to look for the owner.

As I was standing fueling up the jet ski, I looked down the short dock, and there came a portly fellow, about 5'2", weighing 300 pounds solid. He had short black hair and no neck that I could see, and he squinted at me through colored glasses. He looked like the bad guy in a mafia film.

I handed him my business card and introduced myself.

"Glad to meet you," he said. "The name is Winnie."

I immediately liked him. And at least his name wasn't Sue.

I shook his hand. "Glad to meet you, Winnie." (No, I did not laugh.)

"This thing is kind of like a snowmobile, isn't it?" Winnie said.

I agreed that it was, more or less.

"You got to come up to Port Huron for the winter snowmobile marathon," Winnie said.

Winnie, a friend of a friend . . . but don't call him Sue

"Winnie, I do not own a snowmobile."

"No problem," he said. "You come up, and I will see to it that you have a unit."

Just like that. He'd just met me, and he'd invited me up to join 100 snowmobiles for 1,200-mile seven-day run from outside Detroit to Mackinaw City.

"What if I took you up on this offer?"

"I'm hoping that you do."

"Then I will," I said sincerely. And I would. Sounded like great fun.

"Where you headed now?" he asked.

"Back to Port Huron City and onto the Detroit River and then out into Lake Huron."

"You don't have to go all that way to get to Lake Huron," Winnie said.

"No?"

"Just stay west on this river for about two more miles down. You'll see a small cut on the left, and that will take you out to Lake Huron."

"It's not on the charts."

"No, but it's there. With this jet ski, you got no problem with depth, and you won't have to face a current. It'll save you about an hour."

Somehow I knew Winnie wouldn't steer me wrong. Marina people always shot straight. I checked the charts again and the GPS. Nope, it wasn't there.

But the idea had appeal. Something not on the charts or on the satellite system.

Why not?

I waved goodbye to Winnie, hoping to see him the following winter.

I headed west on the small river. About two miles down, sure enough, there was an inlet, of sorts. "Small" was not the word for it. It was a ditch—a long and straight ditch maybe three feet deep and four feet wide.

What the hell, let's go for it. I took the ditch and hit 45 miles per hour. It was great. The jet ski buzzed over the ditch, eight inches off the ground, straight as an arrow, with the bushes flying by me inches away. Tree branches whizzed by my head. Flanked by trees and foliage, the Bumblebee and I shot down the ditch.

But then I saw the end and Lake Huron coming up. I slowed. That was something else again. I stopped the Bumblebee and got off and walked to Lake Huron. It was like looking at the ocean. The last 25 yards into Lake Huron were a small gully wash maybe three feet wide and two feet deep with a pebble and sand bottom. Then it opened up into a 20-yard beach at the end. It was like coming out of the Amazon onto an empty beach that no one knew existed. I walked from the center of the ditch down to the deserted beach. I looked up and down the empty beach of Lake Huron. No one in sight. I walked back to the ditch again. I did this three more times, back and forth.

I had a plan. Back the Bumblebee up about 40 yards, open up the throttle, and hopefully the momentum would push the 1,000-pound Bumblebee out like a cork in a champagne bottle. We'd skid over those last 20 yards right into the lake.

Of course, if I didn't make it, nobody was there to call the ambulance.

I decided to do a test run. I put a stick in the ground to mark the spot where I had to back it down or go for it. Then I got back on the Bumblebee.

The adrenaline was pumping when I went back 40 yards and stopped and turned it again. I throttled it up and let go. It hit 60 miles per hour in seconds. I saw the stick marker coming up fast. I stopped. It all went perfectly.

I turned the Bumblebee again and went back up the ditch 40 yards. Again, I opened it up. Hitting 60 again. Coming down the ditch full blast. There was the stick. Past it! No return now. I was skimming the surface, barely touching water. If I hit ground or shifted too far left or right, I knew the Bumblebee would stop dead, and off I would go like a rocket. But no turning back now! I hit that last 20 yards like a bat out of hell. At 60 miles per hour, I had the momentum. I fixed my eyes on Lake Huron. What I did not expect was the small sand hill in the water the last two yards. I hit the small bump. The Bumblebee became airborne. Nothing could stop 1,000 pounds moving at 60 miles per hour. We took off like a cannonball headed for the lake. Pow! The Bumblebee and I landed right in Lake Huron, still together. A big smile took over every muscle in my face. Too much fun!

For such moments, life was made, and this made life for the moment. Priceless!

Chapter 6
The Happy Bumblebee Rider: Lake Huron through Lake Michigan

I came out of Port Huron and headed up the eastern shoreline of Michigan on Lake Huron to Harbor Beach. My first reaction to the landscape was surprise. The beauty of Lake Huron stunned me. The water was crystal clear, blue and turquoise, some of the cleanest water I had seen in all my travels. I could see down into it for four feet or more. It might not have been Tahiti, and I couldn't see any lovely maiden out there with me, but it was a northern paradise.

Then I came upon those white beaches of Michigan. Those wide, pristine beaches went on and on, mile after mile deserted and unspoiled. It must be one of the best-kept secrets in the world of tourism. The clear water lapped those white, white beaches in the same way, it seemed, that it had for centuries, long before we came around. Either the folks of Michigan had decided to keep the white shoreline dream their private pleasure, or the tourism board was falling down on the job. If it was the latter, let's hope they don't hire a new board that decides to be efficient. Sometimes there are advantages to folks goofing off on the job.

As I traveled north on the new waterway, the terrain kept changing. I was aware of boulders on the shoreline but unsure of how far out they went or how big they were. I was testing my distance from the boulders when I hit one. The Bumblebee bounced right off. Nothing broken. I looked around. Lots of boulders. I pulled the jet ski up and stopped and took out the paper charts to study them. The charts told the story. Lake Huron had a shoreline that stretched out three to five miles, with hidden boulders, shallow spots, and shoals. So I could either run the shoreline and risk cracking the hull or go out into the safer, deeper waters. I fired up the jet ski, and out into the deep waters I went. Offshore was the answer, but I missed seeing that gorgeous shoreline.

The first part of the day was nice; I ran at about 35 to 45 miles per hour. I was still cautious. These were new waters, and I didn't feel comfortable in them yet. At about 10 a.m. the winds changed, coming in from the southeast, which put the two- to three-foot waves on my backside, and that slowed me to 25 to 35 miles per hour.

Despite that, I made it to Harbor Beach by early afternoon. The marina was small but close to the city. There had been so many beautiful, quaint, or striking little and not-so-little towns on the trip. This was another. Could you get saturated with pretty? No, not really. Each new town and marina was a delight. When I walked down the street, each person I met made eye contact, and, even knowing I was a stranger, each said "Hi." I grinned in reply, "Hi." I'd never met such friendly people. I also noted a sign that read: "Bad Axe High School." In the context of such a friendly place, the name was amusing.

I walked by a store called Brennan's Men's Clothing store. Outside there was a wooden sign saying they made custom T-shirts and baseball hats. That pulled me in. Inside I met Sheila, Lisa, and Stacy. They were

Brennan's: Fabulous customer service and good looking shirts to boot

wholesome and smiling and hard working. It was impossible not to like them. I introduced myself, and we all hit it off 100 percent. I explained the trip. Surely such a trip needed its own T-shirt and baseball hat. We worked on the logo and design. We came up with my e-mail address on a T-shirt. Another T-shirt had the logo of the Bumblebee circled with the words: "Great American Loop." On the arm was my first name. It was the perfect gift to send to all the people who had helped and supported me on the trip.

Though the town was very close to nirvana, I paid the highest fee thus far for dockage at Off Shore Marina—$12. But we must consider all the amenities that were included in that fee—no electricity, no water, no cable TV hookup, and no pump out. However, I did get one cleat. The floating dock was two feet wide and 12 feet long and right by the fish-gutting station and dumpster. For those tricky lessons in balance, possibly the fee was justified. But, to be just, I had to weigh that $12 against all the great marinas and yacht clubs that had given me free dockage. Seen in that light, I was way ahead.

After the balancing routine on the floating dock, I sat down on a bench on land and looked at the map. I had covered 1,576 miles of the Great American Loop. The trip was 27 percent completed. I was pretty much on schedule to finish the Great American Loop as planned. But I still had a lot of geography in front of me. I was a long way from certain what the future held on this trip or whether, in fact, I could complete it. But every time I thought about Jim's gambling pool, I gritted my teeth and went on. Hip Bee had her winnings coming to her.

The next day, June 21, summer officially arrived to the northern lands. It was going to be a great day—65 to 72 degrees. You could not ask for more than that.

I left Harbor Beach headed for Caseville, Michigan, which was on the inside of the thumb of Michigan. The early part of the trip was flat and glassy. I ran about two to three miles offshore because of the boulders. I passed a trawler that was headed up the shoreline as I was. The cruisers onboard waved as I passed them. Though I was about two or three miles offshore, I had few safety concerns with such clear visibility.

About 20 minutes after I passed the trawler, I had only a few seconds before I hit it—a wall of fog. It was deep, and I was in it within seconds. It closed in around me, a curtain of gray. I was offshore by at least two miles and blinded by the fog. Who knew I was there? No one. I slowed the jet ski. The roar of the engine dropped. I wanted to be able to hear other boaters out on the water before I ran into them or they ran over me. But with the jet ski engine sound reduced, would they know I was there? I had to rely on hearing them first.

There was no wind. The water was flat. Just that fog and the silence. I knew I could always turn left and hit land, if I didn't start drifting in circles in the fog. I had never experienced fog like that. I imagined a monster jumping up out of the water to swallow both me and the jet ski. Imagining that controlled my real fear of encountering another craft also blinded by the fog. The latter was a real possibility. And that trawler that I had passed earlier was still on my butt somewhere.

Luckily, the water was calm. But all the identifications that kept me oriented to space had vanished. I was this little cork bobbing in a massive body of water; land and markers were gone. I couldn't see 30 feet around me. The one thing I knew was that the whole state of Michigan was on my left-hand side. But I did not know where the boulders were. Many boats and ships had lost their hulls to that shoreline. Patience, caution, and attentiveness—those were my guides. I also prayed that the satellites were still orbiting and bringing me the vital info I needed on the GPS. Otherwise, there was no way to say where I would end up in that fog. I stopped to get my bearings and check the GPS. It said a lighthouse was nearby.

Seemingly by magic, there it was, materializing out of the fog like an apparition. I looked up from the GPS and saw a structure appearing out of the fog about 30 feet in front of me. There was this massive, impressive structure, and there I was, this little dot on the water, drifting through the fog. The lighthouse looked like a medieval castle in the middle of the water. The base was an octagon of poured cement about 30 feet high, topped by a four-story square brick building with a lighthouse. The bottom 30 feet of cement were gray and made it appear as though the top part of the lighthouse was floating above everything, like a mirage. It took only seconds before I realized I wasn't far from the rocks at the base of the lighthouse, less than 25 feet. And I still had that trawler on my ass somewhere. I started the jet ski and went around by the lakeside.

I later learned that it was the Port Austin Reef Lighthouse. It was at the tip of Michigan's thumb and marked the turning point for northern-bound ships heading into Saginaw Bay. It had been a lifesaver, dutifully fulfilling its 100-year-plus obligation of sending the wayfarer into land. I wasn't lost anymore. It had delivered me from the amorphous world of water and fog.

With my return to the real world, real bodily functions made themselves again known. At this point, I had been in the wet suit for hours.

The bilge pump was full, and the master bladder said "Now!" I pulled down the wet suit to release. I had lost a lot of weight over the course of the trip. I could look down and not see my fat belly; it was a straight shot to the little guy. It was a pleasure to see him again. But have you ever been in cold water all day? Do you know what it can do to your hands and feet? Basically, it had the same effect on the little guy. There was little aim left. Just fire away and hope it hits a general direction. But what a relief!

The trip had made me fit, whether I wanted to be or not. Of course I wanted to be fit (don't we all?) but had never been able to stay with an exercise program. The jet ski offered no options. Either I hung onto the vibrating jet ski and shed some pounds or the journey would come to an end. After riding that number of miles, my body was taking on different shapes, but they were all good shapes. When I left, I weighed 190 pounds—now I was 165, stomach firm, upper shoulders and arms muscular and lean. (Compared to the shape I was in before the trip, I now felt like I was in World Atlas form.) Because I was constantly holding onto the throttle grips, my hands were so strong I bet I could squeeze orange juice from an orange with one hand—peel and all. I figured my hands were weapons of destruction. I must admit I enjoyed the healthy feeling, but to ride thousands of miles on a jet ski to achieve it? Maybe my sanity was now in question. However, it was the best weight-loss program around. For more information call 1-800-Fatjetskiier.

As the fog abated, I headed west to Caseville, where I would visit with Mr. Brian and his family. I had known Mr. Brian for well over 15 years, but this was my first visit to his home state. While I visited with Brian, I also had the Bumblebee serviced at the dealership. Late 40s, outgoing, Mr. Brian was a great host and showed me his community, "the Thumb," and all the great land of Michigan. Clean and beautiful towns. Lovely beaches. Great open land. Friendly people, bad axe or not. Michigan was the place to raise a family. When I explored the shores in that area, I could quickly see it was Bumblebee territory. I had never seen so many in the water. But I came from the South, and it was just too cold in the winter there for me. Ice fishing? No, I don't think so.

The last night in Caseville, I went out with Brian to a restaurant. It wasn't fancy, but Brian touted their fish as the best in town. "Pollack white fish and beer is a helluva dinner, but the morning after can create a smell like a July dumpster." The next day I would be wrapped up in my wet suit. That was an inviting thought. There was a long bar, about 20 feet, and the place had about a hundred people in it. They all knew each other. The pop music was blasting. I smiled as I watched a young woman of about 26 climb up onto the bar on all fours. The young woman picked up the shot glass with her teeth and gulped it down, without touching the glass with her hands. Then she did it again. I joined the applause. There was still something wild in the north country.

On June 23, I was back on the water going from Caseville to Alpena, which was 94 miles. It was a chilly day, so I was back in full wet suit. The morning was clear, with west winds that made for a good run for several hours.

I came upon South Point and rounded it. Once I turned into Thunder Bay, I knew why the bay had received that name. The winds kicked up to between 20 to 25 miles per hour. I had to stay far offshore to avoid the boulders. I heard somewhere that Thunder Bay got its name because of a Native American legend of two lovers who died in the bay. I thought a few times I would join them. It was a fight to get in.

But I finally pulled into Alpena, a welcoming city. I refueled and got back on the Bumblebee and turned the key.

Nothing happened. The Bumblebee was dead.

I tried again.

Nothing.

Damn. Not again.

I tried again.

Nothing.

Hadn't I been there before? Well, it was Sunday, so I had no choice. I'd have to deal with it the next day. I wasn't going any farther that day.

After a needed night at the local Holiday Inn, I was back on the dock the next morning and had the jet ski towed to the local dealership.

The repairman came out and told me the problem: Water was getting in the piston, which blocked the engine from starting.

"But I had this same problem in Wildwood, New Jersey," I said.

We put in another call to the Mother Country. Several theories about the mechanical problem were floated: (1) Water got into the bilge (bottom of the hull) and was sucked into the air intake system; (2) When I throttled up and down really fast, particularly in rough water, the water flowed into the exhaust; (3) "Or maybe you rolled it in the water," the repairman suggested.

"No, I didn't," I replied.

"Maybe you did."

"Why would I?"

"Fun."

"Look at this gray hair. Do you see me doing that?"

"Sure."

I wasn't sure whether I should be flattered or offended.

"Well, I didn't."

"Have it your own way."

"Is that the opinion of the Mother Country?"

"What?"

"That I rolled it?"

But again the Mother Country checked the jet ski all out. Nothing. The repairman ended up pulling the plugs and blowing the water out. After about 30 minutes, it started back up.

"I don't feel that reassured by the Mother Country anymore," I said.

"Were you ever?" the repairman asked

"Yes, I was. In the beginning."

"That was the beginning, wasn't it?"

Odd fellow. Sort of mysterious—like the Great Lakes and the constant mechanical failure of that contraption.

"So I can just keep expecting this?" I asked.

"If you want to."

That repairman should have gone into politics.

"My confidence level isn't high," I said as I left the dealership.

"That's your business."

I felt like my eyes might pop out.

But I was as good a politician as the next guy. "Have a nice day," I said, waving and smiling as I left.

He waved back with a big smile, "You too, buddy."

Back in the water. Off to Cheboygan, Michigan. Past Thunder Bay again and past Middle Island.

It was getting windier and colder, and I was still running a mile or two offshore. In a jet ski, I had no confidence in the present. Why was it just stopping like that? What would happen if it conked out out there? I kept a steady grip on the throttle as the Bumblebee moved to the top of Michigan. That was where the Straits of Mackinaw separated Lake Michigan from Lake Huron. I knew from my charts that I should hit a river before I hit the straits. And there it was—the river into Cheboygan.

The marina was right at the river mouth on the outskirts of the city. At the tip of the land, there was a camping area and a boat ramp. I paid the $5 fee, which was based on an honor system, put the money in the envelope and ripped off the receipt. But it was another mile farther up the river to get to the city. It was cold and nasty and drizzling. I rode the jet ski up and tied off on the bulkhead, which was near the main part of town. I looked around for some kind of instructions on usage but couldn't find any. There was only a sailboat at the bulkhead. At this point, I was just tired and cold from the day on the water. All I wanted was a motel room and a warm meal. I carried my luggage to the closest motel, which seemed like about half a mile, and checked in. I dried off and headed for the restaurant.

After I ate, I went back to the bulkhead to check on the Bumblebee. Low and behold, there was a note on the Bumblebee requesting that I check in at the marina for dockage. That meant I had to walk back to the marina where I had paid the $5. Well, there was only one way to do it, so off I went on foot. I didn't want to take the jet ski and get wet again. When I got to the marina, I inquired about any fee for the cleat usage at the downtown bulkhead.

The young lady said, "That will be $22 for the jet ski."

I couldn't speak. That was $2 a foot. The silence hung between us like a dead fish there on the counter.

"That's the minimum charge for any boat under 21 feet," she said.

"I paid the $5 ramp fee. Couldn't that be applied to the $22 fee?" I produced my receipt.

"No."

"Would you be so kind as to call your boss?"

"No."

"Would you—"

"No."

I studied her. She was blonde, about 20, with strong features, which were now set in stone. I wondered whether she had this battle often. It appeared that she had. It also appeared that she knew this battlefield better than I. Would it help if I explained what I was doing? I did. She didn't care.

Sometimes you had to know when you were fighting the current, and right then I was. I threw in my cards and paid the fee.

"Thank you for all your help," I said sarcastically as I left. Then I knew why most boaters pushed up to Mackinaw City or Mackinac Island.

The next morning I woke up debating my two choices for the next part of the trip over the northern tip of Michigan. Should I go around the Straits of Mackinac or take the inland route? That day it was cold, and the wind was blowing. The inland route was 61 protected miles of a few small lakes and a river. But at the end of the inland waterway there were about 20 miles that had to be covered by land to connect with Lake Michigan. My final destination was Petoskey, on the west coast of Michigan. There was no waterway connector, and I hadn't a clue as to how I was going to make the land connection when I got there. Would there be some sort of lift (trailer) to transport me and the jet ski into Lake Michigan?

Well, if this trip were totally predictable, where would the fun be?

I decided to take the inland route. What a great decision!

My first obstacle of the day was a small lock. It was only about 30 feet long and held only one boat at a time. The lockmaster was young, and he eyed me and my jet ski with a nasty expression. Either he woke up on the wrong side of the bed or he hated jet skis. I pulled the jet ski into the lock chamber. I was holding a thick bungee cord from the top of the lock. The lockmaster opened up the gate quickly. The water blasted in, much faster than I had experienced in previous locks. It was whitewater. He was testing me. I tightened my grip on the bungee cord as the water whirled around me and the jet ski. The jet ski rocked back and forth violently. A few times I didn't think I could hold the Bumblebee and me at the same time. I gripped the cord as the water roared around us. I knew the lockmaster was watching and enjoying this. Finally the water level evened and stopped rising. He looked shocked that I hadn't ended up in the drink. I paid him the $4 lock fee and thanked him and moved forward.

I never knew what his problem was. But then I didn't know what Jim's problem was either, except perhaps he was convinced he'd make some easy money. I'd proven that lockmaster wrong. I would prove Jim wrong, too.

Each time I came out of a lock, it was always a treat. There was always a new waterway, with new experiences ahead. Despite the harrowing experience in the lock, when I came out, I was delighted by the picture-perfect scene. Surely it must have been the "land of Oz." I thought I could easily spend months in that place, west of Cheboygan.

But the day was just beginning, so I moved on. Next time I would not pass that by.

The inland route was wonderful, the best run of the trip. The river and lakes were lovely and sheltered. On Lake Huron and Lake Erie, I'd had to contend with wind and cold waves. Both were harsh and tiring. But this was a calm, tree-lined waterway. Birds chirped in the branches and rustled in the brush. The wind was soft on my face. Crooked River was just like its name, crooked. It was about 50 feet wide, and I traveled it at about 45 miles per hour—skimming down the weaving tunnel of greenery. The river and small inland lakes were just too much fun.

I came to the next lock. After the previous one, I was trying to ready myself for the worst. Again, it was a small lock that could hold only a 30-foot boat. All the previous locks I had been in had doors on both ends. But this lock had a metal door that came down overhead, and it was curved like a shovel. It was unlike any lock I had ever been in. The lockmaster, who was just the opposite of the previous lockmaster, called the lock a "clam," and that's what it looked like. It raised me six inches. I chatted with the lockmaster about what to expect on the inland route.

"Yes, you'll run into a dead end," he said.

"Is there any lift down there?"

"I don't know for sure. Wish I could help."

As I pulled out he waved, "Hey, good journey!"

"Thanks!"

After the lock, I decided to pull into a small marina and ask for directions. As I turned into the marina, a 60-pound swan swam out to greet me. It stopped right in my path. I slowed the jet ski. The great white swan didn't move, fixing its beady eye on me. "Shoo!" I said and waved my hand. It didn't budge. It was acquiring an unmovable battleship quality. I was clearly in his or her turf. "Shoo! Get out of the way!" I yelled. The swan remained stalwart and determined. I could almost hear it talking: "Come on. I dare you." It had made itself perfectly

Bird from Hell

clear with that blasting honk/squawk. Damn. That was one big, mean swan with an attitude. I tried staring it down. No luck.

I smiled and nodded. "Here's to you, pal. I'm moving on."

The swan glared back. No sense of humor there.

I turned back out of the marina. Mother Nature won again.

The marina probably didn't have any directions anyway.

Crooked River dumped me into a wide lake. Every lake had a marina, and, sure enough, I found one. Lakeside Marina also sold Bumblebees, and they were happy to pull me over to Petoskey. The problem of how to cover those last 20 miles was instantly solved. Soon after, I arrived in Petoskey Marina and onto Lake Michigan, the last of the Great Lakes that I would travel.

(Footnote to the great city of Petoskey: There was a section of the city that had such steep roads that the streets could not be cleared of snow and ice during the winter. So if you bought a home in this neighborhood of about 100 homes, you had to vacate your home three months during the winter each year.)

I left Petoskey on June 26 and headed south, down the west coast of Michigan toward Chicago. It was a milestone. Moving south meant

I was no longer going north into those cold waters and wind. Things would get warmer from then on. That day I made Leland. The following day I was out early again and traveled 104 miles. Cloudy skies. The days were ticking by. Me and the jet ski. The beautiful coast of Lake Michigan. The jet ski hummed along. I gripped the throttle. The waves came and went. I was 12 inches from those waves, and they changed every few feet. They changed with the light of the day, the temperature, the depth of the water, and the wind, and they changed with forces I could not see or feel. I watched the waves coming and going, circling around me. Each wave was different. They were like people—fat, slim, tall, easy, difficult, stubborn, and fun. No one wave was like the other, just like people. Some were energetic and cheerful and charming, like the three kids (Chris, James, and Ashley) working at Leland Marina who convinced me to spend the evening there. Some were vigorous and studied, like the young men shooting fish with bows and arrows in the harbor (the water was that clear). Some were charming but businesslike, like the young woman who had just interviewed me for the local TV station. I watched the waves coming and going, circling around me. Some were cheerful and determined at the same time, like the hot dog man in Ludington who had retired and ran a hot dog stand on the weekends. Waves. Each was different. Just like people.

I had a deep tan by then. I stopped at a restaurant for lunch one day. As usual in those small towns, when I walked into the restaurant, the locals stared at me. Why does he have that tan? Is it a tan? Even with tanning spas, Americans hadn't had tans like that for scores of years. As one customer eyed me and frowned, I introduced myself and handed him my card.

He smiled as he read it. "Looks like fun to do this trip," he said, shaking my hand.

"It is," I said with a smile.

"Think you'll make it all the way?"

"I hope so."

"Sure. You can do it."

"Thank you," I said, taking my seat at the table.

The greeting card had served me well during the trip. Suspicion always turned to support and encouragement and curiosity. I hadn't met one stranger on this trip who, when he or she understood what I was doing, hadn't given me openhearted support. Some seemed to want to come with me. All wanted me to finish, completing my dream. Americans always supported a dream. Except Jim, of course. But in his odd way, he was supporting me too because every time I thought about him and his bet against me, I was motivated to go one more mile, one more hour, one more day.

In Ludington I saw fulgurites for the first time. These were glass shapes made by lightning. When lightning hit the sand, the sand was superheated and created glass forms. With a greenish cast, each fulgurite was different and resembled an actual lightning strike, as though each stroke of lightning had created its own definite, lasting record of its brief existence.

While in Ludington, I reserved a motel room for the coming night in Saugatuck, Michigan, because I'd been told rooms were hard to come by. Little did I know that I'd just created an unexpected wave to hit me when I reached Saugatuck!

Farther on, I stopped at the Saugatuck Marina. A lovely young blonde woman helped me with my dock slip. I asked whether I could pay her to take me to my motel. We got in her Chevy convertible and hit the nearby highway headed to the motel. There I was, a guy with gray hair and nothing but a jet ski, being escorted around town by a young blonde. Did I feel great!

"Do you mind if I ask you a personal question?" she suddenly asked as she drove, the blonde hair whipping back from her soft features.

"No, ask away."

"Are you gay?"

"Are you a lesbian?" I retaliated.

She didn't speak. The air was definitely colder.

"No, I'm not gay," I said. What had made her think that? Just because I was in good shape didn't mean I was one of the queer folk. I sat up straight in the car seat and cleared my throat with a deep growl.

"I didn't think you were," she said, the wind whipping through her hair. "But do you know you're going to the Hangar Motel?"

"And?" I asked, mystified.

"It's an all-male gay motel."

The wind whistled by my ears. I smiled because I didn't know what else to do.

"Such is life," I replied, pretending to be cavalier.

She eyed me with doubt. When she let me off, she gave me a worried look. Who knew what fate might await me.

After checking in, I walked quickly into the motel room. I put my bag down and immediately called my mom. (I must say here that I couldn't care less about anybody's sexual choices, but, because it wasn't my sexual choice, I was taken aback for a while.)

"What's wrong?" she asked, hearing the tension in my voice.

"This is an all-gay motel."

"A what?"

"A motel for homosexual men," I explained.

"In Michigan?"

"Yes! And, no, Mom, I didn't know it was when I made the reservation."

"Is it dangerous?" she asked.

"I don't think so. I don't know."

"Is anybody hitting on you?"

"Mom!"

"Rock Hudson was gay, I think. I didn't know that until after he died. Did you know that, son?"

"No."

"I even heard that Cary Grant was gay. But I just don't believe that."

"Mom, you're no help."

"Here's my advice, son."

"Yes," I waited, peeking outside through the curtains.

"Put a chair up under the doorknob tonight. That'll slow those sex maniacs down. You are awful cute now with your tan and losing that weight."

"Good night, Mom." I hung up.

No, I didn't put the chair under the door. And I never talked to Mom about it again. But as I walked the town that night, I wondered where my 85-year-old Mom had picked up all that tabloid information. I'd never seen her read a tabloid. On the other hand, she was Hip Bee of the Internet. What was she doing on the Internet for all those hours anyway?

Saugatuck, Michigan, was truly a wonderful city and very eclectic. There were numerous little novelty shops, restaurants, and artwork everywhere. They even had a chain-link ferry that took you across the river. The chain-link was hand operated with a true chain that was hand wound and attached to each embankment. All boating traffic

The chain link ferry in Saugatuck, Michigan

yielded for the little ferry. Yes, I would say Saugatuck was a keeper, and I would stay at the Hangar Motel again.

I got a ride back to the motel with a local taxi and made arrangements with the driver for him to pick me up in the morning. The next morning he was there right on time, and I left the Hangar Motel, my reputation intact. I told the taxi driver about the Great Loop adventure. He was so intrigued he took me to breakfast and paid for it. After a misadventure in which I thought the Bumblebee was stolen, I came back to the same dock mechanic I had seen the night before. He knew I had spent the night at the Hangar Motel. The blonde had told him. He wouldn't look me in the eyes. I wanted to say, "But I'm not gay." But the right moment to say it never arrived. To just blurt it out would have meant opening up the subject. The guy definitely didn't want to talk about that subject. The hell with it. I let him keep his delusions. They seemed to bring him some joy.

I was on the water again. On that day the wet suit came off. The sun was out, and the weather was perfect. I'd been cooped up in a wet suit for 37 days. You could not imagine how nice it was to simply piss off the side of the ski without having to hassle with the wet suit. After all, there aren't any pit stops or Shell stations out there. Then, I got that first cold splash of water on my bare skin. It knocked the wind out of me for a second. But it was not enough to make me put that wet suit back on. It was just too liberating to be out of that rubberized container for a while. I looked almost human again.

I was coming upon a point again. Points were land extensions that jutted out into the water. I had come to hate points on Lake Huron and then Lake Michigan. When going around the points, I always hit the roughest waves. Around I went again. Again, rough waters. I cleared the point and kept moving. The worst of that day's trip was over, I figured.

That day I was going through the time zone change from Eastern to Central time. I was watching my GPS to determine the exact moment when it would happen. Would I get some spooky effect? For some reason, God knows why, I'd been thinking about the Bermuda Triangle that day (maybe too many points in one day). Just as the time change came, a rogue wave came out of nowhere. It was two to three feet high on flat Lake Michigan. With that, I kicked the Bumblebee up to 55 miles per hour and scooted onward to Michigan City, Indiana.

The beaches were filling up with people for the weekend, so I decided to ride 100 yards off the coast. I spotted an inner tube floating offshore right in my path. I decided I should investigate. It was probably just a tube that got caught by the wind and was heading out for the deep of the lake. I slowed down as I approached. Two lovely legs were sticking out over the tube. Then I knew there must have been a problem; I would assist this stranded soul back to shore. Pulling up to the tube, I was shocked to see a young woman floating along, tanning herself, topless.

"Are you all right?" I asked, somewhat stunned. She could see it in my eyes.

"Yes," she smiled.

"Would you like my sun block 45?" I asked the beautiful mermaid.

"I have my own. But thank you."

"You're kind of far out. For an inner tube."

"You're kind of far out yourself. For someone from Virginia," she smiled, noting my registration plates.

I introduced myself.

"My name's Lisa," she said with a smile.

Let's leave that episode there.

Subject: Wher's Larry NOW!!!!!!!

From: <waverider4222@palm.com>

Date: Sat, 29 Jun 2002 23:03:23 +0000 (GMT)

To: <all@all.com

Well the last general email was from Caseville, Michigan,,, my wireless Palm pilot has not picked any radio waves this far north,,,but I am in Saugeatuck, Michigan on Lake Michigan, in the lower southern corner,,,,total miles todate 2,206.4 (GPS they are great),,,Since it has been awhile I will try to remember what has happened. Everyone on this email knows me via work or friends, and most people considered me an ass-hole (well at least as a boos at work ,I was the one that always said NO), well that has been cured with the 2,000 plus miles on the jet ski,,,(I think it ///the physical asshole//// has moved to another location on my body),,, for the GUYS,,,Michigan women,,,they have big HONKERS, blue eyes,blond hair,,,where do they get those hood ornaments? (milk and berries, and honey I guess),,,,speaking of berries,,when I walk through these towns or step into a bar,,,everyone stops and turns and looks at me,,,seems odd,,I think it is the dark tan, Michigan folks are fair skin,, Yes this will be the last of the Great Lakes,,look forward to getting into the rivers,,no wind or wave issues,,,well keep those letters coming,,and go by the web site,,,oh I have to move now getting cornered by the gay guys HELP!!!!!,,,sidebar,,,it is not pretty when you are traveling at 55 MPH and run into a bug swam,,your face gets the bug pits (just like the car wind shield) and you do not see them coming at 55 MPH,,,also one thing I will leave you with if you are considering the jet ski trip in Northern Michigan (water is cold) so on cloudy and windy days I wear a full wet suite, gloves, hood, and boots...have a good day

larry

I arrived at the marina in Michigan City the next morning, June 30, at about 6:30. As I approached the jet ski, I noticed a note on the handlebar. I picked it up and unfolded it. The note had been written by some kids. "Go wave rider!" What a wonderful encouragement! The fact that kids had written the note made it all the more special. Maybe Larry and his Bumblebee had helped some kid believe in his or her dream and that it could be fulfilled. I hoped so.

Feeling high from the words of the kids, I left the marina soon after and headed to Chicago. It was a smooth, uneventful last leg of the Great Lakes journey. Chicago was a milestone for me. I was 2,245 miles into the trip.

Approaching Chicago was an awesome sight from the water. It was Sunday and about 90 degrees. Sailboats, yachts, and pleasure boats dotted the harbor. It was a vastly developed and well-kept harbor. The skyline of steel and glass rose before me. Hundreds of boats were docked in rows along the harbor, cars streamed along the lakefront drive, and the air was alive with the bustle of a vital city.

Chicago has one of the largest metropolitan harbors in America. I had detailed charts and book information of the Chicago Harbor, but I still wasn't sure of my location or direction. At one point, I just sat in the middle of the harbor and pondered my surroundings. A nearby boat was tied to a mooring in the open harbor. The couple onboard yelled

The Chicago skyline

for me to come over to their swim platform. They were Chicagoans and could not have been any nicer. They tied me to their stern and fixed me a glass of cold tea and asked me about my adventure. They fed me lunch as I talked about the trip, and then they gave me information about the harbor. What a welcome to the Windy City!

Later, I pulled up to the exclusive Chicago Yacht Club. The dock boys could not have been more helpful. They were kind enough to put me under a dock and out of the sun because all the slips were taken—it was Fourth of July week, and downtown Chicago on Sunday was packed. So for me to get a little space out of the way was like finding gold.

The taste of luxury was just around the corner. I hailed a cab over to my new accommodation for the next few days. The Swissotel was somewhere between three and four stars, but when you got that many stars, who cares. It was first class, but you could imagine what I looked like coming through the door. Picture a guy who is wet, smelly, sweating, in bathing trunks and T-shirt, carrying several tote bags, and wearing flip-flops. But I did have a credit card that passed muster. The bellman hustled me off to the 29th floor and a view overlooking the Chicago Harbor. It was my first real break since leaving Buffalo and entering Lake Erie. I would stay in Chicago until July 3. The hotel staff told me that the room was reserved for the Fourth for the view of the fireworks display.

After having room service, I decided to venture downstairs to the local hotel tavern. I wandered over to the bar and stuck my head in and noticed nothing but men everywhere. That seemed odd to me, so I decided to ask the bell clerk what was with all the men in the bar. I should have known. That day was the Gay Pride Parade in downtown Chicago, and it drew people from all over the area.

"I understand completely," I said. After all, I was an ex-Hangar boy myself.

Subject: WHER'S lArrY now

From: <waverider4222@palm.com>

Date: Sun, 30 Jun 2002 23:37:51 +0000 (GMT)

To: <all@all.com

Well I am at Chicago, yes,,the windy city,,(not windy) 90 degrees,good winds, no waves,,nice beaches (just did not know they had beaches on the Great Lakes, even through I enjoyed the Great Lakes and all it's wonderful people I will be glad to get on the rivers where the wind will not be a factor with the waves and my little jumping cork in the water (jet ski), total miles 2,244.8 or 39% completed, I am guessing St Louis will be the half way point. I feel like the little red cabouse (I think I can, I think I can). I am lucky in Chicago I have a friend named Tim who has done all the posting of the pictures on the web site (special thanks to him), he plans to take me out one night to a place called WEEDS, he has a bunch of friends that are named Tim, so whenever I see Tim and he is with other people, all I say is "Hello Tim" odds are with me 80% of the time that there will be a Tim or Timms in the group,,,,I will only stay here about 2 days, way to much stuff to do in Chicago, and it is to big of a city for little country home boy. I stayed at Blue Chip Hotel C! asino last night in Michigan City and went to a place called Matey's ,,,it was Saturday night and the place was hopping, bar built over top of the restaurant outdoors, to much fun,,and the people in Indiana are great ,,,as the guy who drove me back to the marina this morning "I had more fun than hair on a Taco."

larry

After that, I met my northern connection "The Tim." Tim had been creating the Web site that held all the pictures taken from the adventure up to that point. He was also the contact for supplies that had been shipped to me. Tim was a great host. Tim had been to a few taverns or so, and he picked them perfectly: Weeds, Life's Too Short, and Hideout Chicago just had way too much going on for anyone to take in the sights in a couple of days.

I was having a great time. Chicago was treating me wonderfully. Aside from the bars and great restaurants, I went to the largest food fair in the United States, the Taste of Chicago. I had never before seen 1,000 port-o-potties lined up like dominoes, but, thankfully, none fell.

I went shopping to replenish my supplies. As I was coming out of a building with revolving doors, a small woman of about 110 pounds was entering. She entered the revolving door, coming in as I hit the door going out. A true Chicagoan, she hit that door like she was coming out of a snowstorm and it was 15 below outside. She pushed the door so hard that my part of the revolving unit hit me in the back of the head

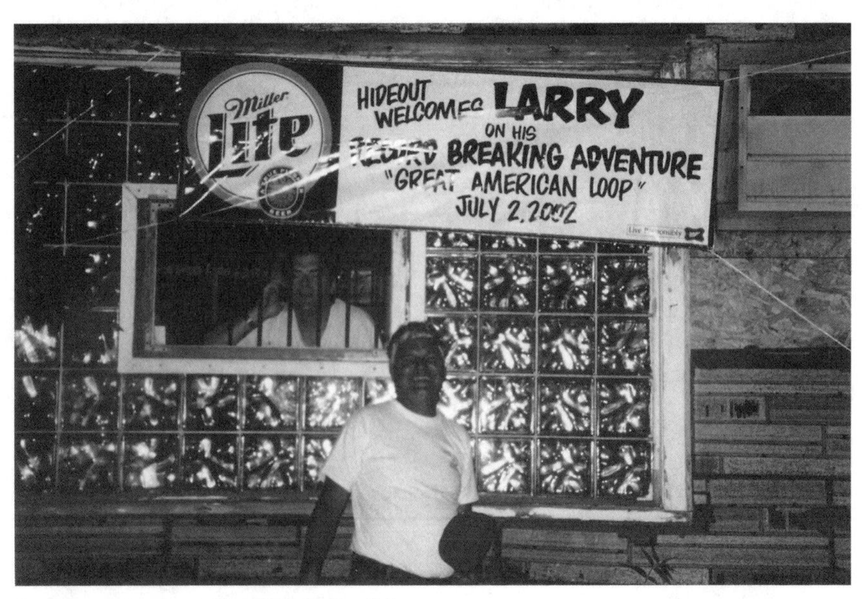

A warm welcome at The Hideout in Chicago

Can you ever have too many Port-o-Potties?

and my flip-flops were caught under the door. Down I went. Right out into the street. I landed with a painful thud. I had just traveled more than 2,000 miles on some of the greatest and most dangerous waterways in the world. I had done it alone on a jet ski. Not one injury. It took a tiny lady from Chicago to bring me down in the revolving door. She didn't stop. I picked myself up with a groan.

Later, I would wonder whether it was a sign of what was to come.

But, aside from the stumble in the revolving door, it was a great time in Chicago. I felt good. I knew that if I quit the trip then, I would not feel bad about myself. Just getting to Chicago was an achievement. The next day I would be curving left and heading somewhat south, straight for the Gulf of Mexico and nothing but warm weather. There had to be a manatee out there in the warm waters, just waiting to be seen.

I would continue. But I would avoid revolving doors from then on.

Chapter 7
Six Great Rivers and Then the Demon Snaps

I left Chicago on July 3 and headed for the inland waterways that connected Lake Michigan to the Mississippi via the Illinois River. From Chicago, I took the Des Plaines River (man-made) to connect with the Illinois River (also changed by man for commercial traffic), cutting southwest through the upper part of Illinois until I connected with the Mississippi above St. Louis.

After the trip was over, I looked back and wondered whether I should have believed in signs. I certainly had had enough to warn me of what might be coming. But of course in real life we didn't think that way. Each difficulty was just that: an individual difficulty that sometimes led to something worse but frequently did not. I had had problems on the trip before, so the initial stumbles were counted as nothing more than that, and, in fact, that was all they usually were. And it wasn't as though I didn't have great moments on that part of the trip. I certainly did. But from then until that "fateful" day on the Tennessee River, I seemed to get more than my share of setbacks. I could laugh and say it was probably that lady in the revolving door in Chicago who started it all, or maybe the gods decided it was time to give me a real test.

It's odd how almost any journey in life begins to have its own shape and its own form, as though it had already been told somewhere. In the beginning of the trip, I was overweight, out of shape, and full of uncertainty. By the time I had circled Michigan on the Great Lakes, I was trim, fit, and confident. Each new challenge—fog, bad weather, the cold—had made me feel stronger and less afraid but respectful. Hour after hour on the jet ski had taken off the extra weight; I hadn't felt that fit in years. Because I was willing to take risks, I had more fun. But those who wish to fulfill a dream should be forewarned. There will come a moment that is more of a test than any you had anticipated. And one you never could have predicted.

More than ever, I was in love with the jet ski. I felt free out there on the water. No one could touch me. I glided over the surface of America's waterways like a dragonfly dancing across the water—a fast buzz one direction, a quick stop, another buzz off in another direction. Each new part of the American Loop presented adventure and surprise. There was sameness at times—just as traveling the interstates could make things seem the same at times. But get off, stop anywhere, and you'd find out it wasn't the same.

I was mostly alone out on the water. Though I made many new friends on the trip, the actual journey was spent mostly alone. I had spent 30 years managing people, directing office routines, and balancing the books. Most of each waking hour was spent with people around me. I was a man who enjoyed people, so that was rarely a problem, but, like most of us, I also wanted my own space and personally defined movement on the planet. I had it. How often had I dreamed of just what I was doing? More than I could count. So, to be finally at the peak of my game, it was a joy.

But trouble started right after I left Chicago on July 3. I was headed for the inland waterways. I was looking forward to that part of the journey. I would be on a river, and wind would not be an issue for a lot of miles to come. Leaving the Chicago Harbor, I once again relished the new and old architecture of a great, vital city. People were bustling to work while I, lucky devil, was enjoying that wonderful city from the waterside.

I was headed for Joliet. Tugs pushed barges loaded with coal, gravel, silica, soybeans, grains, iron, and chemicals; 45 million tons of that stuff went from Chicago to the Mississippi (or vice versa) every year. So you could imagine that the commercial river traffic was plentiful. The barges were heavy, flat, hundreds of feet long, rusted with their many trips through many waters. They had a foreboding quality—huge, lumbering, slow moving, and grouped with four to eight other barges, steered only by the tugboat. These barges reminded me of the spacecraft in the movie *Alien*. Heavy bolts and metal with a massive, industrial-age quality.

I reached a narrow part of the river. Two barges were tied to the left bulkhead and jutted out about 100 feet into the river. Normally this wouldn't have been so difficult to maneuver around. But a tug was pushing two more barges side by side, taking about 200 feet of the width of the river. It was coming at me. That left me with about 10 feet from the left side of the moving barge to the three-foot-high cement embankment on the right. It was a narrow channel to run—cement on one side and working monster barges and a tug hundreds of feet long on the other.

A normal-sized boat would have turned around and headed backward until the barges passed. I sized up the situation. The Bumblebee had room. I throttled it up to 35 miles per hour and rode up the side of the 100-foot barge. I had about three feet on each side of me. (The barges went through the bridges by bouncing off the wood pilings, so I was clear about avoiding that.) Given my knowledge of tug operators, I felt he would not push the barges toward the embankment. I also kept glancing at the concrete embankment, ready to jump off the Bumblebee and over the cement barrier if my instinct about the tug operator turned out not to be correct. If the barges started to move my way, I was ready to jump off and leap over the embankment. My heart was pounding in my ears. The enormous rust-colored metal side of the barge loomed on one side like something out of a sci-fi film. I slipped through the narrow passageway and kept moving at top speed. I doubted whether the tug captain ever saw me. "Balls to the wall or cement or metal."

I went through three water locks that first day. From Lake Michigan to the Mississippi River, the water dropped 120 feet. The locks were now federal locks, built for heavy commercial traffic. These were no longer the smaller, older locks with friendly lockmasters that controlled the Erie Canal.

Brandon Lock and Dam, from a distance, seemed like a one-story elongated construction whose size was intimidating. It was a large project. The gates to the lock were enormous steel structures about 20 feet high, and there was a walkway on top and two steel X's on each gate. Outside Brandon Lock, I radioed ahead to the lockmaster on the VHF and requested permission to enter the lock.

"No," he said.

"I'm experienced with locks. I've been through all the locks on the Erie Canal," I said. The sun was out full strength. It was over 100 degrees.

"No," he said.

"I'm doing the Great American Loop, and I'd appreciate—"

"No," he said. Then he went on to explain that a jet ski could enter the lock only if it was tied to another boat that was going down the Illinois River. "And you have to be on the boat," he concluded. "Those are the rules."

So there I sat. In the sun. Wiping the sweat from my brow. While the lockmaster sat in his safe, small, air-conditioned booth by the gates of the lock. I could barely make him out. An hour passed. I waited. I bobbed in the hot sun. He sat in his cool control booth. I plotted his unexpected demise. And I waited. The heat only seemed to intensify.

I plotted his long, drawn-out death by some exotic form of Chinese torture. I waited. Another hour passed.

Then a boat appeared with two friendly looking souls on board. Both waved in return when I waved. I zoomed up close and introduced myself. Bob and Mary weren't surprised by my problem. "From this lock onto the next two, the lockmasters aren't Americans," Bob said. He was probably in his early 40s, his beard and hair tinged with gray.

"It feels like that, doesn't it?"

"They get their salary from a foreign government. Expect the worst."

I stared at them. Were they kidding?

Bob and Mary were a good-looking young couple, probably in their late 40s, headed to the Mississippi. Both looked like they'd spent weeks on the waterways enjoying themselves.

They let me tie on and ride with them through the lock.

"Were you kidding?" I asked. "I mean, about the lockmasters not being American?"

"That's no joke," Bob said with a big smile that broke through his beard tinged with gray.

"Was it a joke?"

"Virginia, huh? You've come a long way."

"But about the lockmasters?"

"Only two more of those foreign devils to get by," he said with a wink.

Of course I didn't believe the lockmasters were foreign agents. It was Bob's joke. I knew they were probably employed by some federal or state agency. Which meant that they were, indeed, aliens from another planet. Bob might have been deceived; I wasn't.

I unhooked from Bob and Mary's boat on the other side of the lock and zoomed off toward the first marina I could find, Harbor Marina. Later, as Bob and Mary sat on a nearby bench chatting with me, I took a shower in a phone booth. The phone booth had been rigged with a showerhead but no phone. (Just because we've all got cell phones now is no reason to let a perfectly good phone booth go to waste.)

Nothing better than a phone booth shower

The marina gave me free dockage and a ride to a motel. I was glad to check in for the night. There were five more locks on the Illinois River. Would I have to wait hours for each one? I asked questions about the upcoming locks. All information was welcome at that point.

It was July 4 and a great day on the Illinois River. The next lock was the Dresdan Island Lock. That lockmaster had the same attitude, no entry until a boat came along; I would have to tie up and travel through on the boat. Of course I knew what was going on by then. Aliens had taken over the dams and locks of the Illinois River. Why they had settled on that particular set of riverway controls worried me. How could I bring them down? No one would believe me if I told them.

Lacking a starship to combat the enemy, I waited. And waited. From 8:30 until 11:30 a.m. I radioed the lockmaster. But he would not acknowledge that I was calling on the VHF radio. Possibly I needed a universal translator before he could understand. I put down the VHF. It was going to be a long day. My final destination was Peoria, Illinois, and I still had 108 miles to go. I found another friendly boater who let me tie on.

Being the Fourth of July, a lot of people were on the river with their boats. The riverbanks were also well populated with the day's celebrations. I was surprised to see large groups of Vietnamese on the banks. One guy was net fishing in his underwear. (I had lost a pair of underwear in Chicago in the laundry; the ones he wore looked suspiciously familiar.)

The remaining two water locks were controlled by kind and professional lockmasters. I gathered the aliens hadn't gone that far south yet. But I still had to ride with other boaters, who were always helpful. On the last lock, I got a ride with a 21-foot runabout, which was not a large boat. Onboard were four adults, six kids, and one dog. They were all yelling and screaming and barking at once. It was difficult to know which sound belonged to which individual. And, yes, the radio was on full blast. The beer was flowing freely. One of the ladies was large and wore a small two-piece bathing suit; I assumed her soul mate had said she looked wonderful. She walked by me jiggling everything that jiggled (which was a lot). She looked at me as though she knew what I wanted. "NOT." My polite glance away from this startling performance didn't seem to convince her otherwise. I had something much worse than aliens to fear. She continued to parade with a curious smile of self-satisfaction, and the kids screamed, and something barked, and the radio blasted. When we exited the lock, I quickly untied the jet ski and whipped away, happily leaving the echo of their fathomless joy behind me.

Peoria, Illinois, was my last stop for the day. As I pulled in, the river harbor was filling with boats and all kinds of watercrafts in preparation for the fireworks that night.

Too tired for fireworks and looking forward to an early bedtime, that night I e-mailed my friends. Knowing I had to check in and communicate with these partners in the journey always lightened my spirits. It was good to know there were people out there in cyberspace who cared about where I was and what had happened that day. Possibly they were living vicariously through me; that was fine. But it changed the feeling of a day to sit down after the day's journey and tap in the latest updates. And e-mail I received usually made me smile or laugh. In so many ways, all those e-mail pals were with me on the adventure.

Subject: Wher's LaRrY NOW

From: <waverider4222@palm.com>

Date: Fri, 5 Jul 2002 03:35:04 +0000 (GMT)

To: <all@all.com>,

Well I am in Peoria,IL.,nice hotel "Hotel Pere Marquette" downtown Peoria, for the firworks on 4th of July,,for those traveling on jet ski on the Illinois River,,,It is fantastic, not clear water but clean,,,watch out for the tugs, they push 3 barges 100 feet long each and 3 aside giving them a width of about 120 feet total, they can take some river out of the river and it is double trouble when there are some barges tied to the shore 2 abreast,,at one part of the river it was skinney,,,I have 10 feet between me and the barge and the cement embankment wall (my jet ski is 11 feet long),,,I had to run about 360 feet down this thin wall of metal with tug pushing,,,comment,,,do not,,I repeat do not get close to the tugs,,,the back wash from the props (wheels) put off major current within the water (stay away),,you have been warned,oh and the odvious, stay out of there way and do not run out of their sight,,,make you safe and they will be happy,,they can not stop (on a dime like you a nd me) those barges once they get moving . I saw my first Beaver today (not sure if it was male or female) ok,,,I have been in the water too long,,,this beaver was not scared of anyone or thing,,,He/She controled this particular spot (neat looking animal),,yes he/she will be on the web site in a few weeks, comments there are 8 locks on the Illinois River, 2 of them are not recreational boat friendly,,,Brandon Island lock and Dresden Island (Dresden is the worst),,, they will make you wait 2 and 3 hours with no traffic in the lock (hum attitude issue) all the others have been very nice,,note for jet skiers,,you must tie up to the back of a recreational boat , get on board to go through the locks,,,a saftey issue, which is ok,,,but I have been through 38 locks and never ask to debark my craft, oh well those are the rules so live with it (no problem,,,tell all hi!,,feel free to pass this email to others, and keep those encouraging emails coming ,,,they keep me going ,,,travel todate 2,414.6 miles or 42% completed out of 5,800 miles,,,looks like St Louis will be the half way point,,, maybe I will stay a few days and toast myself,,,(HIGH FIVE MYSELF)

larry

The following day I woke up not feeling well. Maybe I'd had too much sun the day before. I considered staying in Peoria another day. After stalling around and getting a late start, I finally decided to go ahead and get on the water and put some miles in. I saw the last lock approaching. I didn't want to face it. I anticipated another long wait and tie on with an obliging stranger.

Surprisingly, the lockmaster allowed me to enter and lock up under my own power. He advised me that guidelines had been issued on lock-through for jet skis, and the gist of it was the jet ski could enter but then you had to climb the ladder and hold the jet ski with a line from the cement embankment. How did I know what the rulebook said? I didn't. I had to take his word, which, of course, I did. I had no choice. I wasn't sure whether he was an alien lockmaster; I suspected he might be, but there was room for doubt.

The stretch from Peoria to Havana was wonderful, quiet, and scenic, with very little boat traffic. The river shores were rustic and attractive, and lots of people were camping out. It sure looked like a nice way to enjoy the Fourth of July weekend. It was a small slice of God's country. It was mostly flat, with thick green trees along the river.

There were stretches of Illinois that could seem very long at times. Periodically the river took on a lakelike quality. It could be wide and shallow with little moving current. The western part of the Illinois River just kept getting prettier and prettier. The banks of white sediment outlined the flat river. The willows bowed down to the shores; the green was intense and invigorating. I knew I was starting to head south again—where the foliage was so much richer. Illinois had, surprisingly, a lot of rivers and lakes.

When I came into the Havana Marina, I saluted the town and myself. (Hmm, I wondered how it was named Havana.) Total mileage now 2,459 miles, or 42 percent completed.

The challenge of that part of the trip began the next day. That challenge? Fuel. There were long distances between stops. It was 120 miles between Havana and Grafton, with one fuel stop available, if it was open. I would be pushing the jet ski to the limits to make it. Until I reached Paducah, Kentucky, fuel was the constant challenge.

Plus the jet ski was still acting up on me. It just would not start sometimes. In fact, it seemed to be doing it more and more often. Each time I stopped, I wasn't sure whether it would restart. I didn't relish being far between fuel stops and the jet ski not starting.

The LaGrange lockmaster was a surprise. He was nice. I called him on the VHF and requested admission to the lock.

"No problem," he said.

I stared at the VHF. Could I be hearing right?

"But it'll be about an hour and a half. There's a tug and barge in the lock heading east now," he explained.

"Thanks," I said.

He suggested I wait on the bank and he'd call when all was clear. There was an old barge by the shore. It had obviously been left there to rot. A willow tree was growing out of it. I tied up to the barge and

FCF "Funky Circus Fleas" Barge

sat down under the willow. Someone had used a nail to etch in the metal surface these inscrutable words: "FCF Funky Circus Fleas." Graffiti. Who could say what it meant to the locals? I enjoyed the pleasant view and gorgeous, warm summer day.

I felt a small itch and scratched. I watched the clouds float by. Another itch. An hour later I was jumping around and scratching every part of my body. Now I knew what "FCF" meant.

The lockmaster called me on the VHF. "Hey, mister wave rider, you can come on in the lock. By the way, what kind of music are you listening to?"

He and his pals had been watching me with the binoculars.

I dove right into the river to get rid of the fleas.

About 70 miles farther on, I came to a fuel stop. At least I was told that's what it was. It looked like the bed of an old truck floating on a few boards with a large cylinder tank on top. On the side of the old truck walls was handwritten "GAS." It looked like something out of the Great Depression. The age of "slick advertising" hadn't touched that section of the river.

I tied the Bumblebee to the barge that had a 25-degree tilt. Beggars couldn't be choosers. Who knew when I'd find gas again on the river? All self-service, no marina greeters—hell, no marina.

I didn't normally stop for a real lunch, but that day I did. My information book gave the restaurant high praise, so I decided to try it. It was on the waterfront with large glass windows and about 10 tables. When I walked in, about 50 senior citizens were already there, seated and eating. Several gray heads turned suspiciously in my direction. I was sweating and covered with river water and extremely brown by then. My clothes were stained with the brown of the river water, and I had white zinc oxide on my nose to protect it from the sun. Through all their sets of glasses, they knew immediately I had come for the shakedown. Forks and spoons stopped in midair.

I signaled the waitress and asked her to seat me outside in the 105-degree heat. I hated geriatric judgments. You couldn't explain because they usually couldn't hear. You couldn't get angry because they meant no real harm. You couldn't challenge their collective wisdom because there were more of them than there were of you. If they knew what I

Gas of last resort

was doing, I would have been a guest speaker at the next AARP meeting, and their collective wisdom would have concluded I was nuts.

But it all turned out for the best because that's where I met John. He was also a Bumblebee owner and enthusiast. John was tall and thin, in his mid-30s, with thick blonde-brown hair and a mustache. We hit it off right away and decided to make the run to Grafton together. Grafton was where the Illinois River connected with the Mississippi, just above St. Louis. I'd received a call on the cell phone to take the jet ski in for a recall of some sort to the dealership in Grafton. So while I waited on the jet ski, John showed me all the local sights in Grafton and found me a marina and a hotel. The Ruebel Hotel was two stories, brick, and looked very much out of another time in the history of the Midwest. You expected to see John Wayne walk out with a six-shooter. But instead of John Wayne, I saw a moth with a six-inch wingspan, a wooden Indian, an outdoor jail, and a pottery store in the old granite Grafton Bank building. Being in banking myself at one time, I particularly noticed how so many old bank buildings were now used for other businesses.

John was a great host there. And it was the first time I'd had since leaving Virginia to just sightsee and play on the jet ski. John and I cut

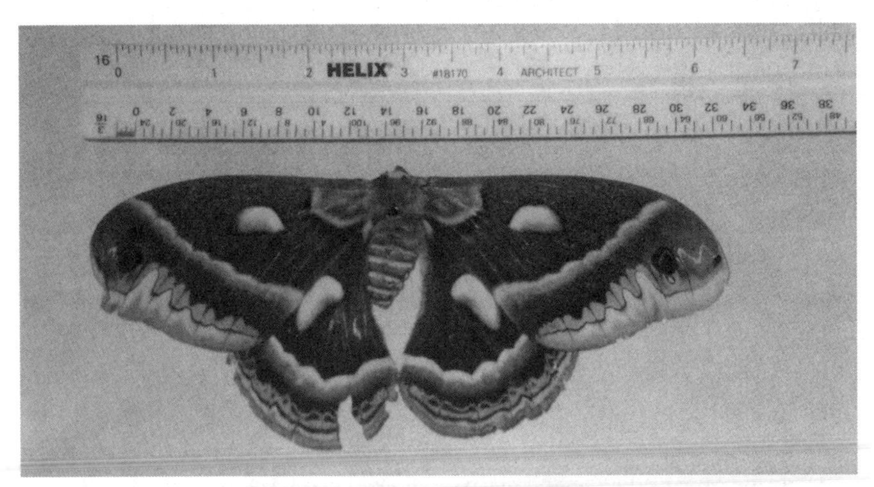

Mothra, the butterfly—how would you like this to land on you in the middle of the night?

through the waters around Grafton, carefree. That particular area had lots of islands and boat rafting where the river sand had built up. Everybody on boats on those July days was enjoying all that the water had to offer.

Subject: Wher's LaRry NOW!!!!

From: <waverider4222@palm.com>

Date: Mon, 8 Jul 2002 21:53:53 +0000 (GMT)

To: <all@all.com

Well I am in Grafton ,IL,,,I have been out of cell (wireless) communication) for a couple of days,,Grafton is a neat place,,staying at the Ruebel Hotel and Saloon,,,,great place , great people,,,jet ski is in the shop getting normal service (plugs, oil and filter change before I go futher South,,grafton is at the intersection of the Illinos River and the Miss River,,17 mile north o St Louis.,,, great trip from Peoria, Il,,,traveling fast had to make 250 plus miles. Stop in havan ,Il, little marina called Tall Timber Marina,small but new in construction,,super folks, I pulled up to get gas, before I finished fueling they had me a Motel room and "Mr Harcum your free car awaits you",,me being stupid, how do you not know that I might steal this car,,,no problem ,the car cost $5,000 and your jet ski cost $10,000,,,(hum boy I catch on quick). Nice place,,,moved on next day had to visit another Lock on the IL River,,"La Grange Lock" the last one on the Illinois River (if you do not know what a lock is ,,,check the Internet , you have homework),,I hated the idea of dealing with another mean Lockmaster,,,what luck,,,he was GREAT ,,,he informed me that it would be about and hour and a half, he had a tug and barge in the lock and that takes time,,he was very pleasent and fun to chat with over the marine VHF,,,so I pulled over to the embankment whaere a small barge was under a tree (shade0,,,I walkup on the barge and rested out of the hot sun,,,hummmm,,,I saw etched by a person with a nail on the top of the barge "F C F" ,,what is that,,"under it it read "Flying Circus Fleas",,,humm sounds strange, about an hour goes by and I am itching to death,,,can not see the little "Bast____",,,thank heavens the Lockmaster calls me on the VHF radio and says come on into the Lock,,he says "Why are you jumping around on the barge ,,,you have a radio and doind some type on dance" I realize he is looking at me through spyglasses,,,GREAT, made his day,,,jumping white dark tan boy trying to dance like Michael Jackson,,,stop at one marina, (well marina is stretching it) it was in the middle of NO WHERE, house , mud,and a barge with a round tank,said "GAS" in white spray paint,,,not in artist hand-writing ,,,but it served a purpose and I thank them for being there for me,,,Stop to have lunch on the river,,,which I normaly donot,,,but this day was a long stretch about 100 miles and no one to smile at,,,well you can imagin me walking into a restaurant,,,average age was 80,,,me dark tan ,river water on me,zinc oxide on my nose,they were shaking in there boots,,,they knew i was going to shake down the place,,,so ,,,to make everyone happy and be able to digest their food I ate outdoors ,,in 95 degree weather,,,and they all smiled,,,there I meant John,,,he joined me on his jet ski to travel to Grafton,got me a hotel room,dinner and a marina,,,helped me get the ski to the dealership,,and gave me all the local history "what a guy,,thanks John" I will not forget,,,last story,,he took me out to a restaurant /bar "FAST EDDIES" famous in it's own right locally. Ate and drank a few beers had a great time ,,even a great band,,,he dropped me off back at the 22 room hotel yet the "Ruebel Hotel & Saloon", well there is not a car on the street (population 600), streets are rolled up,no lights in the lobby of the hotel, and door is LOCKED,,,I assumed my room key would do the trick,, NOPE,,hum,,,I started trying other doors on main street with my key,,,no luck,,,low and behole there is the police station,,,you can imagin me poping at 2:00 AM, knocking on the police station door,,,hummm he had a strange look on his face,,I was cute (for sure) I guess he figured I was turning myself in for some crime and a place to stay,,,he calls the owner,"Jeff I have one of your guest" me thinking GREAT,,owner thinks I have been arrested,,he tells the officer which door on the rear of the hotel has the access door,,,sure enough it worked,,,click my heels "HOME AT LAST, HOME AT LAST" Not sure how my email communication will be over the next few weeks, so hang in there with me,I will survive

My email list has grown to about 150 so please fell free to duplicate and resend to others,,,please understand wireless Palm Pilot has no spell checker and I left my dictionary home,,,, I am also been know to write things as I see them,,and it is not meant to be offensive,,just the facts and nothing but the facts

larry

July 10. Time to move on. My special fuel tanks would be needed from then on. Fuel stops were scarce. Marinas were 100-plus miles apart, and the Bumblebee could get only 70 miles comfortably before it ran out of gas. Special fuel tanks had been shipped from Virginia Beach to Caseville, Michigan, to Chicago, Illinois, and were now waiting for me in St. Louis. I had thought I would need them in each of those places but hadn't, so they'd followed me around the country. But then I did need the tanks. They would allow me to carry an extra 10 gallons of gas so that I could stretch the limit of the jet ski to 110 miles conservatively, maybe 20 or 30 miles past that if required.

John was on vacation and decided to make the run with me past St. Louis to the famous "Hoppies" Marina, where I would pick up the fuel tanks. It was nice to run with another Bumblebee rider who knew the river. John was always pointing out all the history and landmarks of the area. The St. Louis Arch was quite impressive as we traveled past the city. It swung high to a graceful arch on the bank by the river, the tall buildings of downtown right beside it. The arch marked "the gateway to the west."

Below St. Louis we decided to stop on the shore where some people were gathered on the beach. Once on shore we started a conversation with these folks who were having a "floater party."

"What's a floater party?" I asked.

They told me. There had been a reported drowning above St. Louis the day before. Because the Mississippi River flowed with such a swift current, early rescue was impossible. Thus, the body would be floating past that point soon. Being locals, they had a fairly good gauge of what time the body would pass. Thus, "floater party." Yes, it sounded sick, but in the big picture, it was a useful party.

I wondered whether I should have asked. John and I moved on.

The famous St. Louis Archway

Later, John and I took another break on the Mississippi, stopping at a restaurant. As we were talking boat talk, a cowboy on a horse walked through the shallow water nearby and stopped and looked at us. He had on a white hat and a red handkerchief around his neck and leather chaps.

I waved hello.

He nodded, as laconic as a cowboy should be. Was I dreaming? Where did he come from?

After a few preliminaries, I got the story. He farmed along the Mississippi and wanted nothing to do with big cities and most of the modern world.

John and I were talking to him and some other boat people and jet skiers. Then about 20 minutes later, I turned to ask the cowboy a question, and he was gone—horse, hoof marks and all.

It was a strange day.

Farther down the river, we came to the famous Hoppies Marina. Because I'd heard about the place since the Erie Canal, I was expecting a big marina with lots of boats. Hoppies was a small fuel stop composed

He's no ghost. He's an actual cowboy working near the Mississippi River.

of several barges pulled together on the side of the Mississippi. Hoppie and Mrs. Hoppie were in their 70s and had been running the place for decades. Friendly, down to earth, their personalities were the draw.

That was where I would say goodbye to John. His brother met him there with a trailer to take the Bumblebee back to Grafton.

John, if you're reading this, thank you for the hospitality. You were a truly great host and historian.

I waited in an old barn by Hoppies for a ride to the local bed and breakfast. The barn was falling apart but still housed a few old boats. I had just said goodbye to John. A strong thunderstorm came up. I was sitting in an old rocker and looked around as I waited. The barn was falling down, hadn't been painted in decades. Where was I? In the middle of nowhere. I knew no one. For the first time on the trip, I felt alone. The clouds boiled up, and the lightning popped. Maybe I had been lonely before, but I hadn't realized it until I'd had a few days on the water with the friendly companionship of John. I felt alienated from everything around me. Memories of the floater party haunted me for a few minutes. That could have been a party for me. Then the ghostlike lone cowboy who had come and gone like a dream. Loneliness could come over unexpectedly. This I hadn't expected. I think it was the shared days with John that made me aware of it. I was sad to say goodbye to my new friend. It would be hard to be alone on the water again. It was a lot of miles before I would come to the end of the trip. I doubted I'd meet another such friend along the way. I was far from my family. I wondered whether I should have called it quits then. The storm shook the old barn, and the rain poured.

But just then my ride appeared for the B&B. There were only three places to stay, and the first two were full. So it was take it or leave it. I had no idea what the B&B would be like. I only hoped it was better than the barn I'd just been sitting in. To my shock, we pulled up to an 8,000-square-foot contemporary house with a swimming pool overlooking the Mississippi River. It was someone's summer home that was rented out. It was amazing. Every amenity was provided, including a player piano and huge glass windows overlooking the Mississippi.

As I put down my bag, smiling at my surroundings, the wonderful housekeeper asked, "The master suite is rented tonight, so do you mind sharing the house with other folks?"

"Is that part of the arrangement?" I asked, pretending offense.

"There will be two girls arriving about 4 p.m."

How old? I wondered. Twenty? Thirty? "I'll have to put up with it, I guess," I grumbled. While I contemplated what she meant when she said "two girls," I tapped out an e-mail to my friends.

Subject: Where's LaRrY

From: <waverider4222@palm.com>

Date: Thu, 11 Jul 2002 00:03:00 +0000 (GMT)

To: <all@all.com

Today was a good day and a sad day, one of mixed emotions, so do not cry because I left Grafton today headed for a place called Hoppies "well known marina on the lower Miss River, (about 30 miles below St Louis)I was told about it many times in the Erie Canal and other boaters, you have to stop,,John , the fellow jet skier rode with me to Hoppies, he has really shown me the greatest hospitality,,, we had two locks to go through,,,no problems ,,they took maybe 30 minutes each,,,no hassles,,got to Hoppies Marina on the lower Miss.River about 30 miles below St Louis,,,Hoppies is a marina of interest,,not your country club boat club,,,but Mr Hoppie is a real boaters gentleman,,,it is a keeper only because he gives out nothing but goodwill to all boaters,,,This is where John and I departed after 3 days of fun,,he will be missed,,he wanted to go futher but money would not allow,,we shook hands and he drove off into the sunset,,Hoppie called a bed & Breakfest

```
for them to pick me up for accomodation, well
I was feeling a little loney ,,,up drives Cory
from the Chimney Rock B&B, she drives me up the
hill, to a spactacular 8,000 square foot house
(contemporary) pool,,unbelievable,,this is a
home not a split up house for rooms to
rent,,she shows me everthing,,great rooms,fire-
places,great place,,,but she tells me that two
NOT one ladies are also coming in tonight to
share the house,,,well I told her that this
will not do, you will just have to find me
another place to stay,,,,then I held that
idea,,,I will wait to see what they look
like!!!!!!!!!!! Stay tuned. I know I will,,,,

larry
```

At a little past 4:00, two lovely young women walked into the house. They were both teachers who got the stay in the house as a gift. My homesick feeling evaporated. We shared drink and conversation and laughs. Some things are better not repeated, but let's say my spirits were uplifted for the next day's journey.

The next day, July 11, I left Hoppies in Kenwick, Missouri, at 8:30 a.m. (Not bad, considering the night before.) That day I would need the extra fuel tanks to reach Kidd River City Fuel at Cape Girardeau. From that point on, the fuel problem was serious.

The upper Mississippi River had tremendous river barge traffic. One barge was 35 feet wide and 135 feet long. One tug often pushed 24 barges, four across and six deep. There were acres of barge coming up or down the river with a single tug. Each tug and barge created turbulence for at least a half mile after you passed it. If you've ever doubted America was hard at work, take a trip on the mighty Mississippi.

About halfway into the run, I decided to the cut the engine of the Bumblebee and let the 15-knot (12-mile-per-hour) current take me downstream and save some fuel. With the time on my hands, I decided to call my daughter on my cell phone. I looked up at the sky as the jet ski floated along and chatted with my daughter for 20 or 30 minutes. When I hung up, I started the jet ski and continued on the river for three or four minutes. But I felt a little dizzy, like a touch of vertigo. There? I was going against the current. The water flowed south, and I was going north. That couldn't be right. I suddenly didn't know what direction I was headed. Yep, you had to wonder, there were only two directions on the river, north and south, and the water was running 15 knots south. I wondered whether I had passed another river while I was on the phone. Looking up at the sky, had I drifted off into it? I didn't know. The banks looked the same, mile after mile. I didn't know. So I was more confused. I knew I had to turn the jet ski around. When I did, I knew I was going the right direction again. I felt so stupid. Too much sun.

I had experienced that on the open seas but not on a river. I decided I needed to keep my eyes focused on the riverbank, to note landmarks that I passed. But how did I get so confused? Maybe I was more tired than I thought. Maybe I had been on the water too long. But I didn't feel that tired. To this day, I do not know why I got turned around. Had some type of vertigo set in? But I couldn't quite believe I had done that—gotten turned around on a river.

The Mississippi was indeed "the big muddy." The water was murky brown. The banks along there were thick with foliage and trees. They were impenetrable. At times it seemed like you had left civilization behind as mile after mile passed and there was no sign of a town or fuel stop or marina. Water debris was heavy from the churn of the tugs.

I was always concerned about cutting off the engine if I was not at the marina. I was not exactly sure of the miles to the next fuel stop, so I refueled without turning off the Bumblebee. That was almost impossible—the Mississippi River was moving, Bumblebee in neutral, and I was emptying five-gallon fuel tanks into the Bumblebee. The banks of the river were too muddy for me to step onto land, so around and around I went, somewhat out of control.

After 112 miles, I hit the Kidd River Fuel Stop. It consisted of a truck parked at the top of the hill by the river that had a hose going down to the floating barge. Because they had to call to bring the fuel truck out, there was a minimum fuel requirement of 50 gallons. Luckily, a boat was fueling when I arrived. The boater let me fuel right behind him, taking the needed 28 gallons. Again, another boater had come to my rescue. If it hadn't been for his civility, I would have had another 87 miles to a fuel stop, or I would have had to pay for 50 gallons and received 28 gallons.

The friendly boaters were Mike and Linda, and their boat was called *Obsession*, with a banner on the back of the boat saying "Nashville or Bust." They were headed past Paducah, Kentucky. After talking with Mike and Linda, it made sense to go the 209 miles to Paducah. If I got in trouble, they would be there with me. We decided to run the next leg together, which made me feel better, though I also knew I would be dead tired when I got into Paducah.

It was a great run, and Mike and Linda were great hosts. I even had lunch on the *Obsession* while floating down the Mississippi River, the jet ski tied to their swim platform. What a great day. It was another 50 miles on to Cairo, Illinois, where the Ohio River emptied into the Mississippi. Then we took a left turn onto the Ohio and went another 46 miles to Paducah.

It was the land of serious rivers. The Ohio looked more like a lake than a river. In Paducah, four navigable rivers merged. All of them were mighty rivers, or as the song says, "all those rebel rivers." The Tennessee (backed up to form Kentucky Lake) was more than 300 feet deep, as was the Ohio. Barge traffic lined the shores. Long bridges spanned the old and formidable waterways. A new bridge was being completed at Cape Girardeau, but there were not a lot of new bridges crossing the Mississippi. Highway traffic squeezed onto the old narrow two-lane bridges.

My destination was the Big E Marina in Paducah, Kentucky. It was one of the few hotels mentioned in my information book. I envisioned a triple-A marina and a wonderful hotel (the latter was true). It was 6:00 p.m. before I got to the marina. What a shocker! The Big E Marina was no more than four small barges pulled together so the riverboats could dock and fuel. The "E" was a blue neon sign on top of the hotel. The hotel was a large concrete structure beside the Ohio that was built in the '60s, but it had a fortress quality that made it look oddly medieval.

The stairway up from the marina climbed at 180 degrees. The steel walkways were moveable to give with the highs and lows of the river. Pilings at least 50 feet high marked the area. But the hotel was a winner. With more than 400 rooms, it was really a convention center. A 12-mile floodwall protected the old part of Paducah from the Ohio, which had been known to flood miles into the city. Murals decorated the floodwall, and the town had restored many of its original landmark buildings. The town was vital to the quilters of America, I was told. Once a year in April, they poured into Paducah and filled up the hotel where I was staying and all the other hotels for a hundred miles in all directions, 32,000 of them. I, however, hadn't arrived when Paducah was Quilt City, USA.

I took a large room with a balcony overlooking the Ohio River. I sat down with a beer and watched the barge traffic as it moved across the wide and deep river. The sun was setting, and rays reflected off the water. You felt like this must have been happening since time began—the slow-moving barges, the deep roll of a mile-wide river, and the light sparkling off that river. I was now 2,882 miles, or about 49 percent of the adventure completed.

It was July 12, and I was halfway around the Great American Loop. Kenlake Marina on the Tennessee River was the halfway point. After taking the Ohio out of Paducah and then up the Cumberland, I took a cutover to the Tennessee River. (The Cumberland was backed up to form Barkley Lake on one side of "Land Between the Lakes," and the Tennessee was backed up to form Kentucky Lake on the other side. Both lakes were hundreds of feet wide and more than 300 feet deep. The lakes were more than 100 miles long, crossing into Tennessee.) It was a beautiful and almost unknown part of the world. National and state parks dotted lower Illinois and western Kentucky, and the waterways formed their outlines. It was a beautiful, lush, green part of the world that the tourists hadn't discovered in force. Locals hoped they never would, and I could see why. Enormous funds must have poured into the area in the 1960s to develop those parks. The waterway development was mostly part of the giant TVA project. You could only imagine the force of these great rivers before they were harnessed with dams.

While I was on the Cumberland, my bladder was full, so I stopped. I was in the middle of the river and nobody was around. I appeared to be all alone. So I took the opportunity to quickly relieve myself. Unfortunately, I didn't hear the barge coming around the bend in the river because it was being pushed by a tug. The barge was a floating cruise ship with about 100 passengers taking in the beauty of the Cumberland. Well, they certainly got an eye-full because I never would have expected to see the Love Boat on that river. I could hear the cameras snapping and the old folks on board snickering as I pulled up my trunks and off I went, like silk panties. Oh well. All I can do is hope no one had a zoom lens.

Kenlake Marina was wonderful. The marina was in excellent condition with covered slips. The grounds were acres of green lawns, flowers of all sorts, all visited by an assortment of brightly colored birds. The owner was exceptional also and the soul of hospitality. The owner placed me in a covered slip with all the large houseboats. Word traveled fast that I had landed, and the next thing I knew, I was invited to the local yacht club function for Saturday night. I had planned to stay at Kenlake Marina for several days, as it was a milestone for me. By noon Saturday, word had traveled, and there must have been 10 local Bumblebees at my uptown covered boat slip. The local jet ski guys wanted to know all about the trip.

That was where I met Mr. Barry. Mr. Barry was the local Bumblebee enthusiast, known for running the rivers. Barry was full of detailed information about what I would be facing as I moved toward Mobile, Alabama. Barry and I were total opposites when it came to Bumblebee traveling. Barry was the outdoors type and would run maybe 200 to 400 miles per day and then camp out on the riverbank and eat dried foods. He was a Yul Gibbons type, back to nature. I, on the other hand, ran maybe 75 miles per day and enjoyed a good restaurant meal and motel and CNN news each evening. We were miles apart in our approach to Bumblebee trips, but that did not stand in the way of our shared enthusiasm for the sport. Barry was one of those people who you never forgot, and I knew I would not forget his help and assistance, particularly when it came to the rivers I would soon be riding. I was sure there were many great marinas on the Tennessee River, but Kenlake was a keeper for me.

Subject: WhEr'S lArrY NOW

From: <waverider4222@palm.com>

Date: Fri, 12 Jul 2002 12:02:16 +0000 (GMT)

To: <all@all.com>

Just a short email today, figured I better send out now, I believe communcation will get difficult as I move down the Tenn. River and Tombigbee River to Mobile ,AL, yep you can tell America I am on my way to Mobile and Pensacola but only the good people not the Grumpies.,,,,ok go get your US atlas,,I am in Paducah, KY, hum KY is that where jelly is made?,,,Yesterday was a first, ran the jet ski 209 miles, my personal first record (I will NOT try to break that one again). Today is the big day,HALFWAY point, yep, 50% completed or 50% started!. What lies around the corner next, got to be FUN, speaking of, OK for the brave at heart, putting together next years jet ski run, yes, looking for 8 want-a-bees , only people that want FUN, meet and see real America and want to lose WEIGHT and get stronger. Only requirements, take the summer off,jet ski,MONEY,GOAL oriented,and sense of HUMOR "Everyday is Saturday",,,,nothing much to report because I said I would keep this short,,riding down the Miss. River,(current is very strong at least 15 knots), I meant Linda and Mike on a regular boat (how boring), we powered off our units (boat engins) and floated down river,,,,to much fun, exchanged stories,,Linda fixed lunch,yep I got curb side lunch service at No Charge (thanks Linda,no thanks to Mike he sat back and BS with me),maybe I need a woman on jet ski to fix lunch! Is that how that works? Take a lady on board and their only job is to fix lunch,Hell I would do that! (donot take offense Ladies). website has new pictures ,just shy of Chicago,,like to know some feed back, are the pictures anygood? What would you like to see more of? (No Kevin NO NAKED girls) ,I get an email from him weekly saying, "Where's the Naked girls", this guy is a billionair, surly he could buy his own pictures!!!!!!! (LOL),,,stay tune!!!!!

Also I have picked up new people on the email list,,if you want past issues,please feel free to contact anyone on this list and they can get you copies (everyone on this list are GREAT people and would give you their SHIRT for a price).

Again I must repeat, I am limited on email addresses, at 150 (max out),using a wireless Palm Pilot with no spell checker, I must say I just write the email and nothing is political correct so I do not mean to offend anyone,,,please feel free to resend or copy of people

Last Trivia, No I am not the first jet ski to do this, I must give credit to John Moffett who was the first, accomplished it in year 2000 with 5,601 miles, My goal is 5,800 miles, I will pick up the extra miles by going to Key West FL

have a good Saturday

larry

On July 14, I was beginning the last half of the trip. The Bumblebee had sat for a couple days, so that particular morning, it was hard to start. It took a lot of attempts. Meanwhile I worried about flooding the engine or wearing down the battery. But it finally started. I said my farewells and took off for the Tombigbee River. Mr. Barry had told me some stories that gave me some trepidation, but soon I would be on the new river.

It was an "easy rider" day on the Tennessee River. My first stop was at Birdsong Marina, where I watched the process of cultivating freshwater pearls. Afterward, as usual with each fuel stop, I doused myself with cold water before I got on the Bumblebee. I doused myself to cool off from the hot weather and to get the muck off. Again, the jet ski wouldn't start. I was told that jet skis were prone to vapor locks, and there was only one way to get rid of them. I completed the steps to break the vapor lock. That meant I took out a spark plug and popped (turned on the jet ski) one time. That cleared the water out and broke the vapor lock. Then I put the spark plug back in. Afterward, the Bumblebee started on the first crank.

I was back on the water. It was a hot day and perfect in every way, with the Tennessee mountains in the background. The spray streamed out from both sides of the jet ski as I buzzed down the river. The sky was blue, with only an occasional cloud—a glorious day.

My next stop was at Perryville Marina, which consisted of a modern store and restaurant. Again, as was my normal routine, I filled the jet ski with fuel and got something to drink. I rinsed myself off with fresh water, holding the hose over my head, and got back on the jet ski. Again, it would not start.

Cursing under my breath because it was the third time that day, I took the seat off to access the engine and spark plugs. I removed the first spark plug and put it on the pier. I popped the engine one time.

A flash of fire hit me as the Bumblebee exploded. Instantaneously and instinctually, I put my arm up to protect my face. Then I stood up and ran for the marina. As I ran, I yelled, "Cut the fuel pumps and give me a fire extinguisher!"

The marina staff was quick to react, but they would only roll the fire extinguishers out the door. None of them would come out and help. I grabbed one and ran back to the Bumblebee that was by then engulfed in flames. I knew the fuel tank was full, and, if it exploded, the dock and the marina would all go up in flames. I was on autopilot. I didn't know I was burned. I ran back to the Bumblebee and blasted the extinguisher spray into the engine compartment. It took three fire extinguishers to contain the fire and finally put it out, and, with luck, the Bumblebee did not explode.

Everything happened so fast. It felt like hours, but it probably took four or five minutes. Once the fire was out, I went back to the marina. That's when I realized I was burned. My arms and face were black and already beginning to blister. Then I felt the pain from the burns.

"Somebody has got to take me to the hospital now," I said.

Ms. Lisa, who worked at the marina, instinctively volunteered. Ms. Lisa was a young woman in her 30s with pink stretch slacks and a T-shirt and tennis shoes and a great smile.

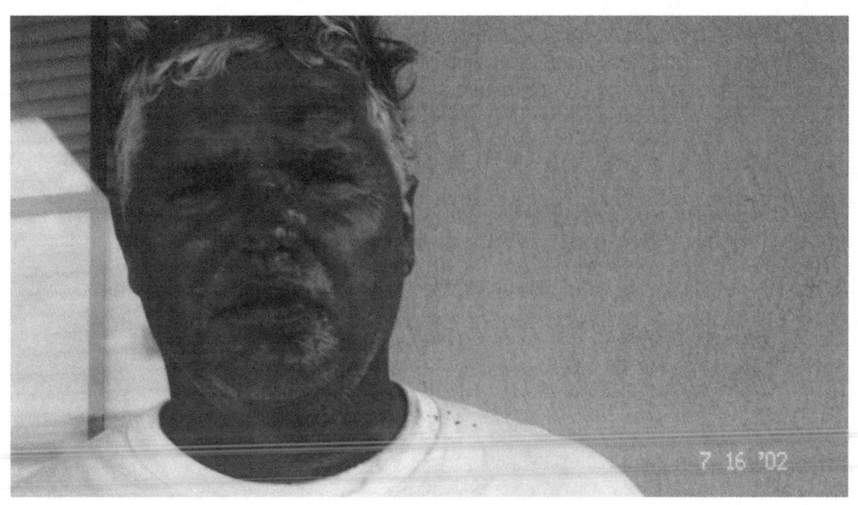

Cute? Nope!

We got into her car and headed for the nearest town, about 15 minutes away.

As we passed the beautiful countryside thick with foliage, the pain kept increasing. Ms. Lisa was shaking with fear. I asked her to tell me a joke.

"OK, there were these two lesbians," she began.

A long silence as the car sped down the highway. She seemed to have lost track of the joke as I winced in pain.

"And?" I asked, trying to keep my mind off my burns and the pain.

"There were these two lesbians," she repeated.

Another silence.

"What happened?"

"There were these two lesbians," she repeated again. She was so shaken she never got past the first line of the joke all the way to the hospital.

But Lisa was truly a savior that day.

We pulled up to the Parsons Hospital emergency room. The nurse had me lay down, and they cut my clothes off. I spent the rest of the day in the Parsons Hospital learning about first- and second-degree burns the hard way. They laid me in cold water for about six hours, and then the doctor and nurse applied cream and gauze. The burns, particularly on the arm I had put up to block my face, throbbed. Then, the pain medicine began to take effect. I was released back to Lisa from the marina. Lisa got my luggage from the Bumblebee. I took a room at Jake's Motel, not far from the marina. It was an eight-cabin motel off the side of the highway. I was exhausted and just wanted to sit down and rest. I was also confused and bewildered from the medicine and the fire. I didn't know what I was going to do about the trip or anything else. I decided I couldn't think about anything until the next day. I lay down in bed and closed my eyes. Into la-la land I went.

Chapter 8
Crispy Critter Rides Again

That night, on schedule, I called my wife as usual. I didn't tell her anything had happened. What could she do? My medical needs were being met. I looked on the map and found a spot farther down the river and told her I was there. She seemed to accept it. My biggest problem was trying to stay focused because the pain pills had a blurring effect on my thinking.

It was a restless and fitful night. The eight-room motel sat off the two-lane highway and next to a gas station and restaurant, but there wasn't that much traffic in the night. I thought the pain pills would knock me out. I tossed and woke and tried to go back to sleep. I felt confused and bewildered each time I woke. I couldn't seem to comprehend what had happened. I watched TV for a while. Turned it off. I didn't want to check my e-mail. Right then I didn't want to hear from anybody or reply to anybody. I tried to go back to sleep. Finally, the pain pills pulled me under for several hours.

I dreamed of a manatee again. I hadn't since I started the trip. In my dream, as in life, I knew one couldn't be far. I was moving into warm waters. Soon, very likely, I would see a manatee. I woke and remembered my situation. I wasn't likely to see a manatee that summer.

The next morning I got up and went to the bathroom. I looked in the mirror. I looked like a monster—my face looked like I had just walked out of a coal bin. My skin was black and red. My right arm and hand were in bandages. Taking off and changing the bandages revealed the nasty-looking blisters. I made some coffee in the motel in the little coffeemaker provided. I sat down with the paper cup of bad coffee. I looked out the motel window to the bright sunny day. It was going to be hot and humid. If I were on the water, it would be a great day.

I had traveled 3,043 miles, with more than 50 percent of the trip behind me. But I was burned over one-sixth of my body due to owner error. Yep, when the spark plug wire lay across an open piston, action would happen. I was stuck somewhere in the western part of Tennessee, and I wasn't even quite sure where that was. The reality of what had happened was setting in. It could have been much worse. I had lived. I would probably recover from the burns. For that, I thanked God. But as I sipped the bad coffee, the depression deepened. I had failed. I had been beaten. I had been through so much. The memories flooded over me. The cold days on the Great Lakes, the 400-plus miles of the Erie Canal, the endless string of motels, all the jet ski problems, all the great people I had met who wished me luck and believed I could do it, and the miles and miles of water I had traveled. I was heartbroken. I had never given up anything before. It wasn't part of my nature to give up. How could this happen? I was in a strange town with no friends. Life seemed small and hopeless.

I threw the bad coffee down the bathroom sink. I went out to the restaurant near the motel. The few customers looked up at me, puzzled and somehow disapproving. I was covered with bandages, and people wondered what had happened but were too embarrassed to ask. I could tell that even the waitress didn't want to wait on the monster, thinking she might catch the infection. I ignored them. After eating, I bought a local paper, and I came back to the motel, which was only a few hundred feet away. Jake's Motel was a well-maintained 1970s structure. There was nothing wrong with the motel. But any motel would have had a desolate, alienated feeling when in that kind of mood.

In my room, I opened the newspaper and looked at a few stories. I didn't know what I was reading. All I could think about was what people would say when I got home. I knew I had every reason to give up. Friends would understand when they saw what had happened, but I knew what they would think. "I knew you could not make it." Of course, they wouldn't say that to my face, but they would be thinking exactly that. A year from then, someone would ask, "So did you finish that crazy trip?" I would have to say no and try to explain about the jet ski fire and my burns. But nobody would really listen or care. Everyone would just look at me with eyes that said, "Oh, you failed." I dreaded it. I had never failed at anything in my life if I had set my mind to it. After all those hundreds of hours on the water, who would guess that it would be fire that stopped me? Thank God I had hosed myself down right before the accident happened. I suppose someone up there was looking out for me.

Jim's self-satisfied expression appeared in front of me. His blue eyes gleaming, his smile mocking and self-important, I could hear him, "It was a good try, but if you can't, you can't, can you?" Jim, who had never dared anything in his life, would judge me. And, worse, he was going to collect on my failure. He'd have the same patronizing smile when he collected from friends who had put down cash in the belief that I could do it. I wondered how much he'd make. Probably a few thousand. I couldn't bear the idea of people handing money over to Jim, the lackluster, who never had an adventurous thought in his life. My blood boiled.

I put on more gauze and changed the bandages. I took another pain pill. Looking at my haggard face in the mirror, I said to myself, "Larry, you've got to accept it and move on." First, I had to tell my wife. Then I had to deal with the burnt-out jet ski still down at the marina and any insurance issues. I had to set up the trip back home. It was time to make all those arrangements and face humiliation. Yes, I had to accept it and move on. There was nothing I could do about it. I couldn't take the fire back or make the burns magically vanish.

Later in the afternoon, I awoke to someone knocking at the door. It was Lisa and a guy from the marina who had stopped by to see whether I was OK. They said they knew a local car rental place where I could get a car, but it couldn't be taken out of the county. I decided to take them up on it and went to rent a car. Having wheels seemed to help. I drove to the local pharmacy and picked up some gauze and medication. Then I drove down to the marina and checked out the Bumblebee. It sat in the water like something that should have been in the local junkyard. There was no saving it. Looking at it made me feel worse, so I got back in the rental car and left.

Driving back to the motel, I thought about calling my brother and telling him. He lived in eastern Tennessee. I knew he would understand and not throw it in my face. It would be logical to go there to recover and not stay in the motel. But reaching the motel, I changed my mind. I didn't want to call him yet.

When I came back to the motel and walked in the room, it seemed small and dark and confining. The air was stale, not fresh and full of life the way it was on the water. I felt like I was suffocating in the motel though the air conditioner seemed to be working fine. I propped the door open.

I watched the digital clock click off the minutes. Finally the hour arrived that I would usually call my wife, Betsy. I had mentally prepared to tell her, but the minute I made the call, I knew I wouldn't. I couldn't. She'd say she had told me not to take the crazy trip. Then she'd be upset and worried. What was the point? All my needs were being taken care of. And my mother had just been released from the hospital after minor surgery. She had kept it a secret from me. I had found out about it through my brother, who had sworn me to secrecy. I had learned all this after her surgery. But I didn't want to upset her. I wanted to be there with Mom when she found out so she'd know I had survived it and would recover. Betsy wouldn't tell Mom if I asked her not to, but Mom might pick it up in Betsy's voice.

"How was it today?" Betsy asked.

"Great. Couldn't ask for a nicer day," I lied. What would she say if she could have seen me at that moment?

"Where are you?"

I had looked at the map and said the name of a place 400 miles farther down the river from the previous night's fictional arrival point.

"You made good time," she said.

"Yes. Like I said, it was a good day. One of the best."

"That's wonderful."

We chatted about various small things—weather at home, a plumbing problem at the house, the challenges with the transition at the bank. I didn't think she suspected. If she did, she wasn't giving it away.

After I hung up, I went back to bed. I just wanted to crawl under the covers for about 10 years.

The next morning was another sunny day. It was my third day in the motel. I told myself to get in gear. The gears were stuck. Was it the medication or something else? I wasn't sure. Not being a depressed type, I tended to blame the medication. Another hot day was coming on. It would have been perfect on the water. I went to make another cup of coffee, all the gloom again descending over me when I looked at my reflection in the mirror. Bandages and burns. That was always the confirmation that the trip was over.

I sat down at the desk with the cup of coffee. Something stirred under the desk. I stood up. There was a small dog, about a foot high, black and white, lying under the desk, sound asleep. It woke and looked at me with mute big brown eyes.

"Hello. Where the hell did you come from?"

I immediately realized it must have come in the night before when I left the door open. It had been in the room the whole time. It had been quietly sleeping under the desk, in the air conditioning, safely out of the 90-plus heat outside.

"You're one lucky guy," I said, "getting out of that heat."

He sat up and perked his ears up. I petted his head. His tailed wagged. I named him Lucky. I was lucky to be alive, and he was lucky to be out of the heat.

He came out from under the desk. I put some water down for him, and he lapped it up. I found part of an old sandwich I'd taken out from the restaurant and fed it to him. He wolfed it down. Then he sat and looked at me with his merry brown eyes dancing. He made me laugh.

"Well, old buddy, if you can carry on with no home and no guarantees about tomorrow, I guess I can, too."

The dog had cheered me up. Life was crazy. It was like some guardian angel put the dog in the room to remind me of what life was

Lucky Jake takes a break in the air conditioning in Perryville, Tennessee

really about. Despite my disappointment and the burns, I was still very much alive.

"I just got to do it next summer, Lucky."

Lucky agreed.

Petting the dog, I took out the cell phone and tracked down a jet ski dealership. Knowing there was probably some insurance action coming up on the jet ski, I didn't want to leave the Bumblebee at the marina. I was probably paranoid. So I tracked down a jet ski dealer who would pick up the jet ski and hold it and then pack it up and send it back to Virginia Beach later.

Then I called my brother. He was a very busy man running for mayor of his town. After I explained what happened, he insisted that, despite his schedule, he would come and get me. He said I had to come to his house to recover. I agreed.

Later that day, I packed up some stuff to send back to Virginia Beach. I included some photographs I had taken of the jet ski and myself after the explosion. It was Thursday, and I knew Betsy was going out of town on Saturday on a business trip. She wouldn't be back until Monday, and regular mail wouldn't reach home until then, when I'd be back in Virginia Beach. She'd know soon enough.

My brother arrived the next day. When I opened the motel door for him, he grinned and said, "Hi, there, Crispy Critter."

It was a needed laugh.

When I was checking out, I asked the motel clerk about the dog that had been in my room. At first she was very apologetic that it had happened. I said, "No, no, I was just wondering whether he has a home."

"I think so," she said. "I'm not sure. But he's been around here for years. He always seems to manage. Just lucky, I guess."

As we pulled away from the motel, I spotted Lucky prancing up the green hill in the back of the motel toward the woods. He was out to enjoy his day, hot on the trail of a squirrel or something equally exciting. So long, Lucky. And thanks.

I went on to my brother's house. It was nice to be in a home, not a motel. I didn't do much but hang out and change bandages and apply gauze.

On Saturday I called my wife. I was surprised because I was sure she'd be on a plane. She'd received the package right before she was getting ready to leave the house.

"What does this mean?" my wife asked the minute she answered the phone.

"What?" I asked, surprised.

"These pictures! What does it mean?"

Did Tim put something up on the Web site? The package would not have arrived until Monday. For years I'd cursed the post office for slow delivery; this time it was fast. No way!

"Explain this, Larry," my wife insisted, enraged.

I couldn't say anything. The silence on the phone was unbearable.

"It was an accident," I said and then explained the whole thing.

"Why didn't you tell me when it happened?" she demanded.

"What could you do about it? It would just worry you."

"I knew something was off when you gave me a town that meant you covered 400 miles in one day. I knew it." She was very angry. "Why didn't you just tell me?"

I explained that I didn't want Mom to know and that she might inadvertently give it away. At first she wasn't buying it. She was too mad. But she didn't stay mad that long. She knew I was dealing with serious burns and serious disappointment about the trip.

"Come home, Larry," she said.

"Yes," I said.

"See your own doctor. Get this taken care of."

"Yes," I agreed.

Luckily a friend was coming from Mobile, Alabama, to Virginia Beach and could pick me up in a few days, and I'd ride back with him.

I picked up my e-mails. Several asked why I hadn't been in touch. Had anything happened?

Subject: WherE'S lArRY NOW??

From: <waverider4222@palm.com>

Date: Mon, 22 Jul 2002 23:17:32 +0000 (GMT)

To: <all@all.com >

My last email was out of Paduca,KY,Must share with you, that morning as I was packing up to leave,I meant JR ,wife and child (14 years old),JR had built his house boat from river floating parts and yes it looked like it, but it was his and it was paid for,(he was a simple guy with black and white ideas),but he wanted to get a picture of ME,,sure enough the wife comes out with a Polaroid Instamatic (you see those at flea markets every now and then),yep he took the picture and we all watched with amazement,,,yes I had to sign it "To JR, may the river debris be with you" Yes the halfway point has been done,,,,and I have to stop and celebrate, Kenlake Marina,KY, the local yacht club even had a party,,great marina,covered slips and mine was under one,,,,the! people are SUPER, yes 2,900 miles and yes there will be more adventures to come.

larry

On day nine after the accident, I was changing the bandages again. The skin was healing quickly. There was much less burned skin to treat, and new healthy skin was replacing the damaged. I looked at my right arm that had been so badly burned. It was healing much more quickly than I thought it would.

Immediately the thought popped into my head. What's today? July 23? If I'm healing, maybe it's not over. How much of the trip was left? Six weeks? Less? I'd be in familiar waters most of the way. It meant coming up much later than I planned, hitting Florida during the hurricane season, arriving back at Virginia Beach in colder waters than I had anticipated, but even those waters couldn't be as cold in September as the Great Lakes had been in June. Maybe I could still do it. I nearly did a jig around my brother's living room.

I told my brother, "I think I can finish this trip this summer."

"You look like hell, Larry. How are you going to do that?"

"I'm healing. Fast. You can see that."

"Better talk to a doctor."

"I'll see my doctor at home. But I'm sure he'll give the OK."

"Crispy Critter rides again!" my brother smiled.

I was so confident I could finish the trip that I began to track down another jet ski for the trip. There were only two companies out there making four-strokes at the time, Yamaha and Seadoo. It was the end of the summer, so I did some calling to track down a Seadoo dealer still carrying the four-stroke. While riding back home with my friend heading up Interstate 80, I made the purchase on the phone. I knew I would be back on the water soon.

And after a reunion with my wife, I decided on the name for the new jet ski: G-Spot.

When I heard that Jim wanted to collect on his bets, I almost lost it. "It's not the end of the summer yet."

"He says you're back, so the bet is settled. He wins."

"The hell he does!" I yelled. "The deal was September 30. We're a long way from then."

"You really think you can do it, Larry? I mean, I've just got to figure out what I'll do with the money."

"Yes, I can do it. Don't you let that bastard collect one cent!"

Because nobody would pay Jim off, he had to settle for the original September 30 deadline. He said he should charge interest because the money was already his. That did it. No way was that guy going to collect.

My doctor in Virginia Beach wasn't initially quite so confident. "I got 30 days," I said to him. "You can see healing. I'll be ready."

"Make an appointment for next week," he said. No commitment there.

The next week I pleaded my case again. I was wrapping much less skin, and new skin had appeared.

"Don't shoot me down here, Doc," I said.

"Make your arrangements. But you've still got to see me next week."

Before he gave the final OK after the third visit, he told me it was a "go" but only with the following conditions: (1) Wear long-sleeve rash-guard shirt; (2) Use zinc oxide on ear and nose; (3) Wear left-hand glove like Michael Jackson.

My wife didn't object that time. I thought she might object more after the accident, but I must have finally convinced her nothing was going to stop me.

I picked August 10 to be back on the water. Halflooper said he was going to join me.

"Don't feel like you have to take care of me," I objected.

"Man, you couldn't pay me enough money in the world to watch your ass. I'm no nurse," Halflooper said. "I want to see some of that water too. I got some time off."

But I still suspected he was worried about me. He denied it, saying, "Hey, I'm worried about me. If I don't get back on the waves, I'm going to go nuts."

I accepted his explanation, only half believing it. But I did look forward to riding the waves with Halflooper again. We always had fun together. Halflooper was going to be with me from Perryville, Tennessee (site of the fire), down to the Florida Panhandle.

We left Virginia Beach at 3:30 p.m. and arrived in Perryville at 5:30 a.m. via car with the two Bumblebees in tow. We checked into a motel and got everything ready for the next day.

I sent off another e-mail that night:

Subject: Where's lArRy NOW!

From: <waverider4222@palm.com>

Date: Sat, 10 Aug 2002 13:27:27 +0000 (GMT)

To: all@all.com

Well like a bad penny, I turn up again ,,,just look under a rock,,,,I will be back in the water again August 12 and that is about 30 days from my BUMP in the road (getting burned) returning to the scene of the flame!!!,,,get your road atlas,,Perryville ,TN ,,,thats about 50 miles from the TN. Looking forward to this remaining 2,800 miles,,A friend has joined me ED [we will call him a HALF LOOPER],,,,so company will be nice,he plans to travel about 1,500 miles with me (we will see).Yep,,I am about 480 miles north of Mobile ,AL then into the Gulf of Mexico (salt water), for those that are concerned I have healed within reason from the burns and all is well I think,,thats for the doctors to determine,,it takes about 6 months for burns to totaly heal and! then one knows the damage,,,I have picked out a new face,,"Richard Geer" ,,,Larry Geer,,sounds catchy huh (have to wear my stud T-Shirt), so much for that bump in the road I expected alot of things but catching fire was not one,,,this will be a short email,,because I am not in the water yet so only highway adventures and they are boring,,,,so" I AM OFF LIKE SILK PANTIES" but I did want to leave you with a recipe that is a killer item for breakfest (just call me Martha Stewart) this is for the ladies but you guys can try it if you understand the cooking language,,,I take no credit,,came from the Perryville Restaurant but it is dam good

"CHOCOLATE GRAVY"

5 Tablespoons of white sugar
3 Tablespoons of coco

```
1 Teaspoon vanilla
1 Tablespoon of flour
1 cup of water
```

```
add coco,flour,water together "WISK" (dam if I
know waht a WISK is) together: add vanilla "WISK"
put in microwave for 30 seconds then "WISK" if
need to be thick add 20 seconds to microwave
"POUR OVER COUNTRY BISCUIT" YUM!YUM! the
orginator said you could call her if you needed
help...Perryville Cafe Renee 1-732-847-7552
```

```
As usual feel free to copy this email and for-
ward to those you believe worthy or you just
want to junk up there computer,,,,please let me
end with THANK YOU for all your emails of con-
cern and it gives me great pride knowing that I
have a second chance to finish verus pushing up
daisey from the ground at 6 feet under. The web
site is totaly caught up with me at this point
with all the new and crazy pictures
```

On August 11 we put our jet skis on a ramp out of the sight of the marina. We both jetted into the Perryville Marina. The marina staff came out on the pier and yelled, "No, no, away! No fuel here!" It was all in good fun. I insisted I had to fuel up. They put up their hands as though to hex me off. "You can get a soda. But no fuel! Your money's no good here!" After we got past the mutual kidding, I introduced them to Halflooper. They were genuinely happy to see me again. Thank you, Brenda, Lisa, and Bob—without you, I might not be living today.

Then it was 1:00 in the afternoon, and we had to get moving to make some miles that day. I also wanted to get down the river from my previous point of failure, from the place that had almost stopped me before. The water did not hurt the burns because there were no open wounds. But I had to keep on the long-sleeved shirt and the white zinc oxide on the side of my face and on the top of an ear.

Halflooper learned from my mistakes and wets down before fueling

We took off down the Tennessee River on a glorious day. After we cleared a few miles from Perryville, I was really starting to feel better. We rode together as we had for some time. When riding side by side, we always stayed 50 feet apart and split the river into three sections, with each jet ski having at least one-third of the river so there was plenty of room between us.

We reached the end of the Tennessee River and headed toward the Pickwick Lock and Dam. It would be Halflooper's first lock. It was a big lock. The steel doors went up hundreds of feet and looked like something out of *Star Wars*. Halflooper was going to get his initiation.

We approached the Pickwick Lock and Dam. I got on the VHF and said, "Calling Pickwick Lock and Dam. This is G-Spot."

"Yes, captain, how can I help you today?" the lockmaster answered.

"I'm traveling south and was wondering if I could access your lock today."

"No problem, captain. What size is your vessel?"

"We seem to be breaking up. I should be at the lock in five minutes."

I wasn't going to tell him that I was 11 feet long. If he knew, I had no idea how long we would have to wait. With temperatures in the high 90s, it was too hot to sit out on those waters waiting for hours. Needless to say, the lockmaster was a little shocked when Halflooper and I appeared. He just shook his head and laughed and turned on the green light. (We would repeat that introductory routine through 12 more locks over the coming days. All the lockmasters were amused; nobody took it the wrong way.)

The gates to the lock opened. Halflooper and I went in and moved forward and tied a line. We cut our engines. Halflooper looked nervous with those enormous concrete walls going up on both sides hundreds of feet. The water came in under us. We rose quickly, up 60 feet in 20 minutes. Halflooper had his mouth open the whole way. "Congratulations on your first lock," I said. "There's 12 more before Mobile." That was my fiftieth lock. The horn sounded, the gates opened, and we came out.

We stopped that night at the Pickwick State Park Lodge, a fantastic place to stay overnight. I had completed 3,115 miles of the journey. More important, I was now certain I was back on the trip.

The next day Halflooper and I went through six locks; one had a drop of 85 feet. We started on the Tennessee River and then made our way onto the Tombigbee River in Alabama. The Tombigbee paralleled the Mississippi going south. It was a truly wonderful river. The 103 miles were from a picture postcard.

That afternoon we stopped at the Midway Marina in Aberdeen. Again, I was back in the South, with all its well-known hospitality. My accent didn't stand out anymore. I was entering familiar ground. The people were first class.

The next day (August 13) we started out early. I had thought it would be impossible to top the previous day, but I was wrong. The run to Demopolis, Mississippi, was a 143-mile trip of a lifetime. If there ever was a perfect day, that was it. The river was 300 feet wide. The sky was crystal blue, with a few white puffy clouds and a bright sun. The river was perfect glass. The river mirrored the sky; at times I couldn't tell the difference between the two. I had remounted the eagle from the first jet ski to the front of the new one. Wings spread, its silver form glided in front of me. That day it seemed as though both of us had taken flight because the water was the mirror of the sky; there was no difference. In a picture I took from the jet ski that day, it looked as though the jet ski had taken flight into soft white clouds. And for a while, I genuinely felt I had joined in flight with the eagle through the white billowing clouds, into an endless blue horizon. It was heaven.

That afternoon we came into the Demopolis Yacht Basin and stayed at a waterfront motel. There we met Jim, "King of the Tombigbee Locks." He oversaw the Tombigbee River Locks. He made a few calls and cleared the red tape on the remaining locks that were to follow. Jim, if you are reading this, thank you for the beer. And thank you for making me change my mind about Jims. Some Jims are decent folk.

Heaven or Earth?

The next day (August 14) was a record breaker—236 miles from Demopolis to Mobile. There was a wood chip factory along the waterfront at Demopolis. Small chips could get sucked into a jet ski's intake and stop everything. Needless to say, we maneuvered through with caution. Aside from the people we saw at the locks and marinas, very few people could be found in such a rural area. The bugs proved worse than the wood chips. But nothing could destroy the beauty of the Tombigbee River. It wound lazily to the south through a virginal, untouched landscape of deep green and colorful birds against a blue sky. It was intoxicating.

When we hit Mobile Bay, the wind was kicking up, over 25 miles per hour, creating three-foot waves. It was saltwater again. It was a sobering jolt after spending days in freshwater on the Tombigbee River. Suddenly we were out on rough water and an expansive stretch of it. We crossed the enormous, choppy bay, looking for fuel. We finally spotted a small marina just as the gauges were hitting empty.

The next day we were tired from the long run of the previous day. We started out late on August 15 and headed for Fairhope, Alabama. After an interesting few hours in Fairhope (where outdoor plants were king), we moved west, with winds pushing at 25 to 30 miles per hour. We weren't far into the run when I looked to check our position on the GPS mounted by the handlebars of the jet ski. The GPS wasn't working. I signaled Halflooper. The government controlled the GPS. Why had it been cut off? That hadn't happened before on the entire trip. We immediately assumed the worse. Halflooper called his daughter on the cell phone and asked her to turn on CNN. No war. What was wrong? We went to the backup navigational charts. With 30-mile-per-hour winds and three-foot swells, charts were a problem for a jet ski. It was impossible to keep the charts dry and stay on course.

After four hours, we connected with the Gulf Intercoastal Waterway. It was like being back on a river—flat and glass and quite a treat. I would always remember those beautiful white sand beaches.

That night we stayed at Orange Beach on the Alabama-Florida state line.

I sent off my e-mail:

Subject: Where's lArRY NOW!

From: <waverider4222@palm.com>

Date: Thu, 15 Aug 2002 06:55:55 +0000 (GMT)

To: <all@all.com

Well back in the water, yes dropped back in the water at Perryville Marina,TN with new jet ski and healed to the point doctor said GO!, Finished Tennessee River and moved onto the Tombigbee River which runs through MI and AL for 470 miles. What a surprise, on a serious note the Tombigbee River is a diamond in the rough, truly one of the preattiest rivers I have been on,and what a way to finish the inland rivers, if I had only on chioce to jet ski,,the Tombigbee would be it,,,nature at it's best and totally unspoiled . Halfloop (Ed) and myself ran the Tombigbee in 3 days (my personal longest day 236 miles). Completed over 3,596 miles or 62% completed or 38% remaining. The Tombigbee River is very unpopulated,with the x-ception of the locks and the few marinas, I saw 25 people on the entire 470 miles. Nothing much to write about but mother nature and Gods gift to America (The Tombigbee River) ,the people at the locks and marinas were fantastic,,,could not help enough,,,last note ! about the locks, there are 12 on the Tombigbee, if you travel the river, be aware of locks that close due to repairs required,,,we were lucky, we missed a lock closing by one day,,,when they close a lock,it shuts down all river traffic for all barges and boats headed the north or south so the marinas get lonely for business. Last item,,,lots of nature and flying birds chasing flying bugs and flying jet ski rider hitting BIG BUGS at 50

```
miles per hour (hurts),,,,new jet ski gets 5.8
miles to the gallon. Currently in Mobile ,AL,
moving to the Florida panhadle next with the
golden beaches

Larry
```

We could walk to the famous FLORA-BAMA bar. Sitting on the state line, half the bar was in Alabama; the other half was in Florida. All the brunettes sat on the Alabama side, and all the blondes sat on the Florida side. With this simple directive, we could always tell what state we were in. Halflooper couldn't decide which state he liked best. He went back and forth all night long in a delighted frenzy. After all, Halflooper was colorblind.

Meanwhile, I talked with a couple who gave me a note to give to a cigar vendor in Fort Myers Beach, Florida. Said vendor was to give me the best cigar made. I had no idea how we ever got on the subject of cigars, but I kept the note.

The famous Flora-Bama bar

The next day (August 16) we had a long, good run to Pensacola, Florida. We ended up that afternoon at a condominium across from a beach, the Dunes Hotel. I had to get the GPS working. Because we were planning to travel the Panhandle around Florida and we would be out in open water where we couldn't see land, a working GPS was vital. I called the GPS manufacturer. They gave me two choices—ship the unit back and it would be repaired or buy a new one. It was Friday, and we planned to leave on Monday. No time to ship anything back for repair. First I had to go to the marine store to buy a new GPS. The new one required that I reload all my preprogrammed electronic charts from a PC. All my maps were at home on my computer. I called the chart people who knew who I was because I'd bought charts for the whole East Coast and Midwest. Using a hotel computer, I was able to download the maps to the GPS off the Internet.

Subject: Where's LaRrY NOW!

From: <waverider4222@palm.com>

Date: Sat, 17 Aug 2002 23:32:49 +0000 (GMT)

To: all@all.com

Well in Pensacola,FL or as locals say P-Cola, but lets backup,stopped in Orange Beach which is in Alabama,but the reason is the Florabama Bar,WILD is the best description,half of the bar is in Florida and the other side is in Alabama,you can tell which side is which by the ladies,brown hair girls on the Alabama side and the blondes are on the Florida,,Halflooper (Ed) who is traveling with me for a few weeks is color blind so he was lost all night, sure enought big girl jumped Halflooper,Halflooper is 200 pounds but big girl was 270 pds,,,boy she put a LIPLOCK on him,no taking him away,love at first bump,glad he has a 3-seater jet ski,,,he will need all of it..... set your travel plans for next year if you like this type of thing,,the largest Yard Sale in the

U.S. starts at Covington,KY to Gadaden,AL on route 127, 450 miles from 8/2-to-8/10,,,Well about 2 years ago I was going to purchase a floating Tiki Restaurant motorized barge and bring it to Va Beach,well could not get perm! its but why I bring this up,,I was running the jet ski from Orange Beach to P-Cola and sure enough running in the water was the boat "KON-TIKI" FROM CHICAGO,IL ,,,,(talked to the KON-TIKI via VHF radio) felt a kinship to it, but real neat to see it under power headed to it's new home ,,yet some investors were moving it to it's new home in Sarasto,FL,,humm there investment has just started,,, Lastly I would like to share some of the song titles from the band at Florabama,"She Put A Liplock On My Alabama Porkchop", "Tequila Makes My Clothes Fall Off", My Baby Is A Seafood Platter", and Went To Bed With A Mermaid Woke Up With A Manatee",,,you can get there music at the following website,, www.rustymchugh.com,,,,worth the $20.00 for a CD,,,Well P-Cola awaits me,we are at a fantastic small hotel Dunes on P-Cola Beach (keeper),,,, This is for Larkin (who is on this email list) Everyday is Saturday!!!!!

repeat if necessary

larry

The Kon-Tiki-Dee

The rest of the weekend in Pensacola was relaxation and chores; even Bumblebee marathon runners had to have clean clothes. Total miles 3,689, or 64 percent completed out of the total of 5,800 miles. What would the remaining 36 percent be like? I knew each day would bring something different. Each waterway, marina, and city brought new experiences.

After a couple of days, I was ready to get back on the Bumblebee. Being on land always made me antsy after a while. But I also kept thinking of that September 30 deadline on the bet. Granted, I had time to get home, but who knew what I would encounter or how much time might be consumed by what I could not foresee?

So off we went. The 107 miles from P-cola to Panama City were perfect. Because it was Monday, there was less boating traffic. That run on the Intracoastal Waterway (ICW) to Panama City was one every jet ski owner should know and experience.

August 20 we headed west from Panama City on the Gulf. Fuel was becoming a problem again. The landscape was undeveloped and rural; we filled up whenever we could. We made Apalachicola at 9 a.m. When we stopped at Caroline's Restaurant for breakfast, the lightning started. Usually we didn't get storms with lightning until late afternoon. Some local fishermen at the restaurant thought we should go ahead and go.

So we took off, heading for Carrabelle, distance 106 miles. The fishermen turned out to be right, and the lightning stayed on the backside, but we were always looking over our shoulders for it. We ended up at a motel that had no windows. I felt like a bat in a cave. I kept opening the door to see whether daylight had arrived. Finally, it did.

Which brings me to a new topic. After 66 motels, you develop minimum standards. So, like David Letterman, I developed the following 10 THINGS TO CHECK BEFORE RENTING A MOTEL ROOM

10. No bugs!
9. Room must have a window that opens and a door that closes.
8. Room must have running, fresh water.
7. Room must have toilet and shower in working order.

6. Bathroom amenities must include soap and toilet paper.
5. Matching bathroom towels are not required, but at least two towels are required.
4. Phone and TV must work. The room must not have a pay phone, and the TV must have at least three visible (and free) channels. Remote not required.
3. Electricity in room required with working lamps.
2. Dead bolt on door that locks from the inside required. (This sounds odd, but I once saw a dead bolt on the outside of a door.)

AND THE NUMBER 1 ALL-TIME QUESTION IS:

1. Is the motel a "theme motel," "all gay," or "bisexual"?

I would suggest that you make up a business card with these question already preprinted and submit them for reply before you rent. The Marriott staff might look at you funny but take no chances.

Carrabelle Police Station—simple but effective

Last, if you are at a fancy motel or hotel, always get two (2) electronic swipe cards. There's nothing worse than to be tired, wet, salty, beat like a dog, and exhausted from the check-in and dragging your stuff to the room. Then you swipe your first and only electronic key. It will not swipe. Get two. One that does not work can make you one mean person.

The plan for the following day (August 21) was to go from Carrabelle on the Panhandle across the Gulf to the western coast of Florida and into the Homosassa River. As the crow flies, it was about 142 miles. The first fuel stop would be Cedar Key, about 107 miles. That required that we leave with the gas tanks full and that each carry two extra gas containers, which gave each of us 10 additional gallons of fuel. That also meant that we would have to refill the jet ski gas tanks in the middle of the water to make it to Cedar Key.

We left at 7:30 a.m. The GPS was up and running. It would be the third time I would travel in open waters without land in sight for several hours. Having Halflooper with me made a big difference. Just knowing another fool was doing it with me made me feel better.

It was a beautiful day with calm water. Some dolphins joined us, popping up out of the water with smiles that could rival that of the Mona Lisa. A sea turtle came up to the top of the water to enjoy the sun. It was perfect.

But after about 50 miles, conditions began to change. A thunderstorm arrived. It appeared as a long, dark elongated line maybe five to 10 miles long. On each side there was still blue sky. But we could see we were heading into an ugly thunderstorm. Lightning hit the water directly in front of us. The storm was heading south. We had two choices. It appeared that there was a small opening in the middle of the squall where we could slide through, or we could go north and come around the backside of the squall. As we got closer, the first choice was quickly eliminated. Three waterspouts appeared right in the opening we had aimed for. They twisted up to the sky, spinning gray funnels from the waves. We quickly headed north, around the backside of the storm. That knocked us off course by about 29 miles. Originally it was 107 miles to Cedar Key; now it would be 136 miles until we felt land under our feet. We were cutting it close, not only with fuel but also with the lightning still popping round us. Nothing gives you the shakes like lightning on the water when you are on a jet ski 11 feet long. And we were carrying extra tanks of fuel. But we had no choice but to push on.

Halflooper slowed and put his thumbs down for me to stop. I stopped and came up beside him.

"I'm running out of fuel," he hollered, panic on his face.

"We got plenty of fuel. We'll make it," I said.

"I'm running out of fuel," he repeated.

"Hell, don't stop to talk about it. We don't need to be talking about it. We need to be moving forward."

Come rain or shine, I was going to put some water under that jet ski bottom.

"Just keep moving until it sputters," I said and moved out again. He took off again.

It got rough. The rain was pelting us. The lightning danced around near us. Halflooper put his thumbs down again. His jet ski was sputtering. We had to put some gas in his jet ski. With two-foot waves, it took balance and steady nerves to keep from spilling the gas or getting saltwater into the tank or getting the jet skis entangled. We put some gas in his jet ski. The crack of lightning made my legs go weak. We pushed on. When we got to the backside of the storm and calmer waters, I put some gas in my jet ski.

After five hours, we finally saw Cedar Key. Both our faces turned from tense worry to big smiles. But coming in from the Gulf side gave us no access to the marina. We were trying to find the entrance and eating gas at the same time. The smiles faded. A guy on a Bumblebee saw our problem and came out and led us into the marina entrance. We would never have found the way without his help.

After refueling, we decided to push to Homosassa City, where the Homosassa River dumped into the Gulf. We hit Homosassa City 171 miles later. I had pushed so hard because Homosassa River was home to the manatee. I couldn't wait another day to see one when we had come that close. Homosassa River was fed by spring water; Spanish moss draped from the trees nearby. As we arrived, we could see all the statues to the manatee that decorated the place. The signs were delightful: "Manatee Zone," "Manatee Gallery," and "Manatee Operations Office."

And there were the manatees, swimming through the clear turquoise water. Graceful, gentle, slow-moving, each must have weighed more than a thousand pounds. About 10 feet long, with a grayish-brown body that tapered off to a flat, paddle-shaped tail, the manatees had two flippers in the front. The faces were wrinkled with whiskers on the snouts. They seemed wise old souls as they grazed on plants in the shallow river. Because the water was clear, we had a delightful view of them. They were as gentle as babies. I felt like jumping in the water with them. Before I knew it,

The elusive manatee

The Manatee Pub on the Homosassa River

that's exactly what Halflooper did. The manatees didn't seem to mind. I told Halflooper that the delicate creatures were almost extinct now; there was no need to finish off the species. The manatees were more enchanting than anything I could have imagined. Later we found the Manatee Pub and celebrated the eternal manatee all over again.

We drank to each other's health knowing that the next day at Tarpon Springs Halflooper would have to depart and head back home.

The trip to Tarpon Springs the next day sent us into water full of seaweed. When seaweed got sucked into the jet ski's intake, it ceased to move forward. Every three miles we had to stop and clear the intakes. The intakes were on the bottom of the jet ski, and, in order to clear them, you had to dive over and scoop the grass out by hand. Sixty-four miles took us three hours.

"I am the captain," I declared to Halflooper, "and you are the mate. Your official job is to clear all intakes!"

"What?"

"You want me to go down there? There's sharks down there!"

Halflooper got so good he could clear both intakes with one dive.

"Good work, mate," I praised him in a loud voice. "You're up for a promotion and a medal."

"You buy the beers, Captain," he said.

At Tarpon Springs, 4,125 miles were completed on the Great Loop, 71 percent complete. There I said goodbye to Halflooper for a while. He had to get back to his job. The game plan was for him to meet up with me September 13 in St. Augustine, Florida, and run with me for the remaining trip back to Virginia Beach.

```
Subject: WHERE'S LaRrY NOW !!!!!

From: <waverider4222@palm.com>

Date: Mon, 26 Aug 2002 01:39:07 +0000 (GMT)

To: <all@all.com >
```

Ok, get your U.S. road ATLAS,,,left you at Carrabella, Florida,about 100 miles east of Panama City up around the Panhandle of the Gulf of Mexico,,,well hold onto your panties, briefs,thong or whatever makes you happy,,this is a good story, maybe not for you, but it is one of those adventures you must participate in to appreciate,,,Halflooper is still with me,,,we filled up with fuel and added two 5 gallon plastic jugs extra for each jet ski,,we were going to go from Carrabella straight east to Cedar Kep ,about 107 miles by way of the crow, well just like Gilligan's Island,, we started a 4 to 5 hour cruise,, the first 50 miles was perfect, calm,glassey, just wonderful,sharks,sea turtles, mana-rays, crazy seagulls and yes feeding porpoises,, this was a run where we would not see land for about 3 hours and we would have to fill up the jet skis in the water with the extra fuel jugs,,,sure enough there was a thunderstorm squal, yes complete with water spout, the storm was about 20! miles long and 10 miles wide but packing a punch and it was headed south, our direction,,, hummm, rethink this option,so we headed north on the back side of the storm at 20 miles per hour for the next 4 hours,,not fun,,,but yes x-citing,,, make you think about" WHY IN THE HELL AM I DOING THIS TRIP!!!!!!" needless to say with alot of thanks to the big guy in the heavens plus neptune and all his friends we made it to Cedar Key, and pushed onto Homossa City /River...My goal was to see a real Manatee in the wild,,,yes that was a long day in the gulf for 172 miles sometimes facing 3 and 4 foot waves. Now for Homossa River,,,worth the risk,,YES!!!!! I saw Manatee's , several to be honest,,,what a creature,,,so gentle and swims so delicate,,,worth the trip up Homossa River,well it made my day!!!! Moved on to Tarpon Springs the next day,,,1 the storm left quite a distrubsnce in the water,,,lots of sea-weed,,,if you understand jet skis they do not have props/propellars,,,,,strickly a fo! rced water system that moves the ski along,,so your water intack on the bottom of the ski has to be clear of debre,,well not going to happen in this new enviroment,,, First let me lay the ground rules,,,between the two of us on two jet skis,I was the Captian and Halflooper was the Mate,,, well as the intacks filled up with seaweed someone had to dive over and go under the jet ski to pull out the seaweed,,,well me being the Captian I delegated that duty to Halflooper, I would have done it but who would navagate, I have to look out for the passengers first,,,that being me when I am not the Captian I am a paying passenger and everyone knows the Captian of the jet ski will not go down with the ship,,(unlike fariy tales0 . I was very proud of Halflooper,,,he did his job well, I would never have jumped in the water "Lions ,Tigers and Sharks, Oh My! ".I think that was the last straw for the Mate (Halflooper) he left to go home at Tarpon Springs, dam good help is hard to find,,,will miss the company, dam good sport, he dived in the water to clear ou! t the intacks at least 35 times that day,,,I changed his name from Halflooper to "Seaweed Muff Diver" he was good at the job ; I saw no reason for two of us learning a trade secrets. Needless to say we departed on great terms and he has the name "SMD" I have moved forward to one of the biggest secrets on the west coast of florida,,Cabbage Key ISLAND , it is about 25 miles north of Fort myers Beach by water,,,and it is HEAVEN!!!! There are 6 cottages,restaurant, good music,and cold beer in a tropical setting, just to good to be true (wish everyone was here), would be a great party, your own party island, well finished 4,242 miles or 73% completed and "EVERYDAY HAS BEEN SATURDAY",,, next big jump will be from Fort Myers Beach to Key West ,Floride the southern most tip for me then make the turn to head up the east coast of the U.S.,,,,well what lies in store for me in Key West,,,and YES I will ask what the THEME of the MOTEL is!!!!,,,and if I drop a $5.00 on the ground I will n! ot pickup till I step on gum with my shoe,, As usual ,please forward this email to those you feel would not upset them or understand me as I call it like I see it. Also you will not hurt my feelings if you do not want these general emails,just ADVISE! New pictures are on there way to the web site and some new ones have been posted that were left off

HAVE A GREAT SATURDAY !!!!!!!!!

Larry

The next day, I was alone on the water again, the first time since the fire in Perryville, Tennessee. I was heading for Cabbage Key. Have you ever seen a fish jump three feet out of the water? Have you ever surprised a sea turtle lounging in the sun on the top of the water? Have you ever watched dolphins leaping up and whirling in the air? Have you ever seen a dolphin not smiling? "Every day is Saturday" for all these marine creatures.

Cabbage Key was an island of about 20 acres located in Gasparilla Bay, about 30 miles north of Fort Myers. Six little cottages were quietly nestled on the island. The cottages were surrounded by thick hanging moss. The dock was right off my cottage. I could watch the sunset over the water. The reds and oranges filled the sky and reflected off the water. It seemed like years since I was off the coast of New Jersey and in the cold Atlantic Ocean and heading for the Erie Canal. I remembered watching each of the springs that seemed to arrive as I headed north from New York to Michigan. I thought of the rough water of Lake Erie, the boulders of Lake Huron, the beautiful beaches of Lake Michigan. I could see again the green riverbanks of the Illinois River and the real men tugs of the Upper Mississippi River. Then the great Tennessee River and the vast surrounding mountains. The never to be forgotten beauty of the Tombigbee River and the run around the Florida Panhandle and across the Gulf of Mexico to Homosassa River and now Cabbage Key. What great memories and more to come.

With 73 percent completed, I still had 27 percent more to enjoy, but I knew the days were numbered.

Chapter 9
Home by the Skin of Our Teeth

After Halflooper left, I went on alone for a few weeks. On August 24, I left Cabbage Key and arrived in Fort Myers Beach, Florida, where I decided to take D.K. Dalton up on his offer that he made the day I started the trip back in May. He had said I could stay in his motel free of charge if I made it to Fort Myers. I was going to take him up on it.

At Fort Myers Beach, it took a while to hunt down the motel from the waterside. I brought the Bumblebee up to the Best Hotel from the beachside. I had phoned ahead, and Dahoe (D.K.'s son) came down to the beach with a group of guys to help pull the jet ski up across the flat sandy beach. That was thoughtful. But as I was walking away, one of the guys who had pulled the jet ski said, "Thirty bucks." Hmm. Then a bellman in the lobby whispered, "Five dollars."

When I went to find Dahoe, he had disappeared. A clerk named John said he needed my credit card. That was suspicious. He ran it through with a $600 charge. I objected. John said it was the normal charge for Friday, Saturday, and Sunday.

"But today is Saturday," I objected, not quite sure where Dahoe had gone or what was going on. "I wasn't even here Friday."

"If you'd been here last night, you'd have your money's worth," the clerk said.

I objected. He said I could go to other hotels on the beach, but they would charge just as much.

Maybe there was a misunderstanding. When I got back to my room, I phoned D.K. on the cell. (I didn't dare pick up the motel phone; only God knew what it would cost.)

"I've spent over $600 in 10 minutes," I said.

"No problem," D.K. said. "I'll get it corrected for you."

OK. Then Dahoe called and suggested I use the Best Hotel courtesy car, which ended up costing 54 cents a mile. To make a long story short, when I checked out, I was presented with a $4,000 bill. I gasped, not sure whether it was a joke. John insisted it wasn't a joke, and of course the police could enforce the law. Just when I was getting really worried, D.K. walked into the lobby, laughing, and tore up the bill. That's D.K. for you.

But that wasn't the last practical joke of the trip.

Tim the Second (not the original Tim who was handling my Web site in Chicago) had arranged for me to follow a boat from Fort Myers to Key West. We had arranged it months previously because I had two choices when I reached that part of the journey. I could take the same route as John Moffett—the inland waterway from the west coast of Florida to the east coast of Florida through Lake Okeechobee, a huge lake that sat in the middle of the lower part of Florida above the Everglades. That route cut off the lower section of Florida as you went from the Gulf into the Atlantic. But if I traveled that route, I wouldn't break Moffett's U.S. distance record on the jet ski. By following a boat from

Fort Myers to Key West and going around the bottom of Florida, I would break Moffett's record. But it was a 140-mile run that would require 30 gallons of fuel, and it was out on the water, thus exposing myself to the possibility of running out of gas or having a mechanical breakdown far from land. So I had decided on lining up a leader boat for safety, and Tim took care of that for me.

The captain of the boat I would be following was Mr. John of the boat named *Hammerhead*. The *Hammerhead* was a fine-looking 28-foot boat rigged for scuba diving and equipped with cruise control, GPS, auto pilot, VHF, and radar—the works! Captain John was an excellent captain who did his homework. At more than six feet tall and 250 pounds, he had been an underwater scuba diver doing the hard-helmet work. John looked like Burt Reynolds, and his years on a tough job showed. John was a planner and a double-checker, ensuring that his equipment was in tip-top shape.

Tim was also along for the ride. That should have made me suspicious. Tim was a born jokester. Tim was smaller, about 5'6", with a mustache and

Holding my own pace with the *Hammerhead*

slender build. Tim was the type who would order and beer and say it was on him and then fill it with water, and, if you didn't watch it, he'd pee in it. Tim would set you up in a heartbeat.

We pulled out of Fort Myers at 7 a.m. with calm waters. The *Hammerhead* went first, and I followed. The winds were out of the west at 20 miles per hour with overcast skies. Captain John set the *Hammerhead* on cruise control at 20 knots. I held my own for the first 20 minutes or so.

Then we got out into the Gulf, with waves three feet high. For the *Hammerhead*, three-foot waves were not an issue. But I was getting the hell kicked out of me. Captain John slowed the paced to 16 knots, but he and Tim were quickly bored stiff going so slow. I was not bored; I was getting smashed. They were supposed to keep an eye on me. Equipped with a radar system that would beep if anything unusual appeared, they fell asleep. I could avoid getting beat up by the waves only by staying about eight feet off the *Hammerhead*'s stern. I was buried in water.

When Tim woke up, he went to the railing of the boat and ate some cookies, purposefully letting the crumbs fly in my direction. Seagulls appeared everywhere. OK, I could take a joke. Then Tim took a piss off the boat stern. With those friendly gestures, I fell behind maybe 200 yards and had to throttle the Bumblebee to its maximum to catch up again. After clearing each wave, I was spinning wheels when I landed on the next wave. Following a boat that was on cruise control and riding a Bumblebee with the throttle anywhere between 15 to 30 miles per hour for two hours was not fun.

The last 20 miles it smoothed out, and I had no problems running outside the boat's wake at 30 miles per hour. The 30 gallons of fuel were completely drained as we pulled into Key West Harbor. When we tied to the dock, I was exhausted.

As I tied up the Bumblebee, Captain John slapped me on the back and said, "You're a trooper" and awarded me the official *Hammerhead* baseball hat. Even though it was a public dock with about a dozen people nearby, Captain John said I had to make the pledge. What the hell. Because that slap on the back had nearly knocked me off the dock, I obliged.

"I pledge to *Hammerhead* that I will not whine or complain. I will always drink my first beer when I dock at the end of the day. I will always make passengers pay fuel cost, and, last of all, if a Bumblebee follows me, I will pee off the swim platform just to let him know who is in control." After that, we all drank beer and sang for hours. But I kept a close eye on the beer pitcher when Tim came around, and he drank first.

The next day (August 27) in Key West, Captain John, Tim, and I went out scuba diving. The clear waters off Key West were magical. We visited several dive sites and tried to catch lobster or spear grouper. About five miles off Key West we stopped over a fabulous reef. Captain John, who had been diving for more than 20 years, said he had never seen water as clear as on that day. You could see 20 feet straight down into the water. Captain John and Tim spear fished while I snorkeled with fish bait food. I couldn't help but think how wonderful it was to be in God's great aquarium. The living coral and schools of

A great day was had by all . . . except the lobsters

I always thought this was my best side

Southern most point on the loop for me

passing fish seemed out of a dream. The day ended with a catch of five lobsters and four groupers. That evening, it was sad to say goodbye to Tim and Captain John. On the other hand, too much fun at one time could wear you out.

I stayed on in Key West for three days (August 27–30) to see what fun the city had to offer. The city was quite eclectic in every sense of the word. Between the thousands of tourists and restaurants, the famous Duval Street, and the hundreds of shops, you could not get bored. Oh! I forgot the bars. There was a bar for everyone's taste, from straight to whatever. At sunset, all the waterfront restaurants and bars filled up with people waiting to see the famous end-of-the-day display. The brilliant orange ball of sun descended into the Gulf of Mexico. I was told that I might see a green flash just as the sun slipped into the Gulf. I never saw a green flash, except the one that came from my wallet as I kept pulling out all those green dollars.

From: waverider4222@palm.com

Sent: Monday, September 02, 2002 1:27 PM

To: all@all.com

Subject: Where's LaRrY NOW!

Ok, Key West,,,,very interseting city,,,it is very straight forth,salers of goods or services and touristoes,,,in the middle is city and federal workers. Those chasing dollars and those giving dollars,,,nothing hard about this,,,,gave them my dollars and pesos and moved on,,,,traveling north up the keys,,,,how wonderful Tiki Bars everywhere, I got so Tiki could be spelled in code:

TIKI BAR:, Bars from Key Largo to Key West

IKIT BAR: Bars you should have missed , sounds like "ICK-IT"

KITI BAR: Yes the Gentleman's Club Tiki Bar,,,hard to find in the Keys but well worth the adventure,, this woild be a MALE thing

ITIK BAR: A Tiki Bar that is "IT' s ICK", a Tiki bar with 2 people on it and one of them is you

Next is KEY LIME = KL

KL Colada, rum and something,after 4 you are a flame,after 5 you are a flaming butt,,I saw this in person''

KL Fish sandwich, looked green

KL ,LIME over a door means mens bathroom

KEY over the means ladies bathoom

KL ,Love hummm, missd that one

KL'sKaroke group,,,presenting the 'KLK's '

KL Girls , come with green thong

OK, Holiday Isle is a KEEPER only on weekends,There is rumor that the song from Jimmy B "Kokomo was written about this location ,well if it is not he missed a good choice.

Speaking of BATHROOMS: I have seed them named everything from,roster to chicken,gulls and pelicans,,,but for you restaurant owners what about "WANT-IT" for mens and "GOT-IT " for ladies, well it just makes sense. If there was ever a good saying for the KEYS,,, 'EVERYDAY IS SATURDAY' well headed to Miami next,,,put your dance-en shoes on SOUTH BEACH !!!!!

larry

Traveling the east coast of Florida was totally different from the west side trip, where I did not see land until Key West. The eastern side of the Keys in the Atlantic Ocean takes you right past each key. Riding the Florida Keys on a Bumblebee was truly a treat. Even the robust girls looked enticing in the Florida Keys' sun. On September 1,

I came to Hawk Channel, where there had to be at least 300 boats of all sizes and shapes, all enjoying a man-made sandbar.

The next day I made the short run to Key Largo, where I hoped to do some maintenance on the jet ski, but the dealership had never seen a four-stroke and didn't have the tools for the unit.

So the following day, I took the ICW from Key Largo to Miami. The alternative was to run the Atlantic Ocean. Most boaters would run the Atlantic Ocean rather than the ICW, but I had no choice—a hurricane had made landfall north around Jacksonville. It was churning up waves on the Atlantic side of about four to five feet. Hurricane season had definitely arrived.

I would never know the Atlantic Ocean run, but the western ICW was breathtaking. Most of the 66-mile run was through mangrove channels about 120 feet wide. I rode at 50 miles per hour through that enchanted marine wonderland. The mangrove tree roots formed an intricate web along the shore, and white herons sat on the roots and in the branches as they looked for fish.

Sunday at Hawks Channel. I took this picture from an aerolite plane.

Coming out of the mangrove channels, I moved into Biscayne Bay. I wanted to see the famous Stiltsville homes off Biscayne Island that sat out in the bay on stilts. There were about 10 such houses. I went closer to get a better picture, but the water was shallow, and I sucked up seaweed. There was only one way to remove seaweed.

That's when I saw a shark circling the Bumblebee. Oddly, I wasn't frightened. After all, the shark was just being nosey like me, and it was his home turf. But he wasn't leaving, and I wasn't leaving until I cleared the intake. I needed something to distract him. I had one thing I could get my hands on—several sticks of Slim Jims. I threw them out in the water, and that got his attention. I unclogged the intake in a flash. I might not have been a certified seaweed diver like Halflooper, but I was damned fast.

Off in the distance, just like Emerald City, lay Miami. Miami was quite impressive when you came out of the mangroves. The Miami

One of a few homes left in Stiltsville in Key Biscayne, Florida

ICW was lined with condominiums and large beautiful homes. If there ever were a place where the Joneses competed against the Joneses, that was it. Each house was trying to outdo the other. The smallest yacht was 40 feet. The rest were ships.

At Haulover Beach Marina, I took the jet ski in for maintenance. There was a bad bearing in the exhaust. It would take two days to get a part from the factory. The GPS 12-volt connection had shorted out because of the saltwater. I had two days for rest and relaxation in North Miami. Haulover Beach was the only legal nudist beach on the Florida east coast. When in Rome, do as the Romans. "Not." Total miles completed: 4,603, or 79 percent.

I was starting to get antsy waiting for the jet ski to be repaired. It was September 6, and I could see the end of the month moving up on me fast. I was at the dealership at 7 a.m., and after the part was replaced on the jet ski, I hit the water at 4 p.m. and headed north. I arrived in Ft. Lauderdale that afternoon, made St. Lucie the next day, and the following day headed for Cocoa Beach. There were a lot of old bridges on the east coast of Florida: new high bridges that did not require a bridge master had replaced many of those older bridges that opened and closed for all the large yachts and sailboats.

I slowed to go under an old bridge that had literally been cut off right in the middle of its span. The bridge simply ended in space. It had become a public fishing pier. As I passed under, I felt something tugging at my life vest. I had snagged a fishing line. The fisherman didn't seem to know whether to be pleased or upset. I unhooked myself and waved. He waved back, pulling in his line, with an expression that said, "The big one got away."

Cocoa Beach was a six-mile stretch of white sand with surfers and sun bathers. You could watch a space launch from there. As there were no launches from Cape Canaveral that day, I happily watched a manatee feeding on the sea grass near the dock.

From: waverider4222@palm.com

Sent: Saturday, September 07, 2002 8:21 PM

To: all@all.com

Subject: Where's LaRRy now!!

Well headed to Miami, this run from Key Largo to Miami was wonderful,,,lots of mango cuts (these tress grow right in the saltwater) , like going through a forrest on water at 50 miles per hour,,too much fun,,,Right before Miami is a a little city called Stilt City, they even have a web page. Not much of a city, no roads ,all the homes are in the water on stilts,,,very interesting, yep I took pictures for the web site, sad part I sucked up seaweed here had to go in the water to remove from jet ski intake , but I had to share this space with a 3 foot sand shark , not sure who watched who the longest. Miami was a destination point I needed the jet ski serviced at a dealership (oil change, spark plugs ETC...). The service manager told me to take the jet ski to Haulover Marina and they would send someone to pick me up out of the water via the ramp. Had to spend 2 nights in Miami,,,what a melting pot of cultures (very heavy Cuban),,everyone speaks spanish,,even me after three hours (I just speak fast,,,they think it is some type of mixed spanish, southern and dalbonease. The dealership directed me to SunRise Motel on the atlantic ocean which is the closes motel too Haulover Public Beach which is all-natural', yep you got it, the only legal nude beach north of Miami, (well when in Rome one must do what the Romans do) . Hummmm well I must go x-ploring on Haulover Beach (shell collecting and bird watching) and sure enough I see people, average age 80, so I fit right in, I met a group that had about 40 members of a al-natural club. X-tremely nice people (lots of smiles and false teeth) , I was the only one who could walk 50 feet without a walker so they kept me busy with little errands. I felt like a stud puppy, the ladies were interested about my trip the men fell asleep. They wanted to know about the west coast of Florida. The club wanted to take a weekend trip to a motel with a beach that would accept their "Beach Style" (they only needed towels and rooms). I try to help everyone as an " Anbassador of the Water" so I recommended the Best Hotel at Fort Myers Beach and contact Dahoe' Dalbon on his personal cell phone number, who would LOVE to have the group. This was my way of helping those who help me. We I departed due to afternoon storm but had nothing to write with to x-change names and phone numbers (they travel very light), towels only. Speaking of towels they had some cute saying on their towels "I am with him and I am with him",, " Butt naked",,,"Frontal Naked",,"MasterCard",,,"Visa" and "Discover", the Discover was not that well endowed (3rd card on the block) As luck would have it the stay in Miami was good because a tropical storm Edouard had hit Daytona Beach at 40 miles per hour winds and heading to the Gulf of Mexico. Still moving north, had to stay in the Intercoastal, waves in the atlantic 4 to 5 feet,,,this part of Florida is FULL of NO WAKES, so this made the going very slow,,,, well speaking of slow,run out of words,,,have a good day

Larry

On September 9, I made the 72-mile run to Daytona Beach. The Atlantic was still too rough from the hurricane. Daytona had a 23-mile beach. It was very wide with clean white flat sand. I watched a red 18-wheeler truck driving along the beach.

An 18 wheeler catching some rays on Daytona Beach

From: waverider4222@palm.com

Sent: Tuesday, September 10, 2002 9:10 PM

To: all@all.com

Subject: Where's LArrY now!!!

Well running the jet ski from Miami to St Augustine had to be all inside (InterCoastal Waterway) verus outside in the Atlantic Ocean,,,the Ocean was all north east winds with waves 4 to 5 feet,,running inside there are alot of 'idle speeds" but you get to see alot of the big coastal homes. Well speaking of seeing ,,, my favorite TV channals are, CNN, Headline News, E! , HIST, Weather Channal, HBO (when the movie has brief nudity) full nudity is boring: did you know in the early 1800's when you died they did not have embauming fluid, so when you died it was straight forth,,the question was were you dead : back then people did go into comas and they through you were dead only to wake up in a coffin,,,well a man invented (it is patented) a bell above ground with a line connected inside the coffinto a bell top-side: have you ever heard the saying "bells from the dead ", well it is true, so if you go by a cemetery listen up. Speaking of a great jet ski run ,from St Lucia to Coca Beach was wonderful (average speed 45), did you know the area code for Cocoa Beach is 3-2-1 (blast off) Cape Canaveral, you ever wonder who has 123 , 666 or 999 area code! . Cocoa Beach east coast king of the surfer dudes and the famous RonJon surf shop, I visited (not a keeper).. JET SKI SAFETY Tip, Florida is the worlds greatest marine outdoor capital, when they replace old bridges with high rise bridges (for boats) they cut the middle out of the old bridge and it makes a great public fishing pier. As a jet skier the great thing is you can go into areas normal boating cannot get to,,,so one can go under other sections of a bridge or converted bridges(fishing piers),,,and being on a jet ski one approaches a bridge span slowly and proceeds at idle speed,with all that concentration the item that gets you is the stealth monofiliment fishing line that I acquired on the other side of the bridge,,almost pulled the guys pole into the water, but he got x-cited at first (throught he had the big one; ME!). Middle Florida has these interesting late summer/fall bugs,,, they mate in air and land on you,,no modesty or shame,,and I noticed they just did not pick me,I guess that makes me a witness to the bug love,, not sure of the name, maybe someone knows the proper name,, 'LOVE BUGS',,,Well getting close to the final leg , completed 4,789 miles with 830 miles by the way the crow flies remaining, To put the miles in perspective ,,go from New York to Los Angeles and BACK.

Please feel free to foward this email onward to those you feel are interested, as usual please advise if you want to be removed from the general email.

Web site has been updated, my man Tim has come back from holiday (hard to keep good help)

Larry

On September 11, I left Daytona Beach Marina at 8:30 a.m. At first I was startled to see crowds of people on Daytona's bridge. They stood in silent respect for those who had died at the Twin Towers in New York City. It brought me back to going through the New York Harbor about four months previously and seeing that empty sky above the skyline. Those crowds on the bridge reminded me of what a great nation this is.

Memory to 9/11 in Daytona Beach, Florida

A tribute to 9/11 on the ICW

I arrived in St. Augustine after a wonderful, scenic 51-mile run. There I would meet up with Halflooper again. He was flying down from Virginia Beach, and I'd have his company for the remaining 800-plus miles back. Halflooper had left me at Tarpon Spring with his Bumblebee loaded in the back of a pickup truck. He had hired a guy to drive him and the Bumblebee to St. Augustine, where he dropped the Bumblebee off at the hotel where we would now, again, meet up. There was also a jet ski rally that weekend. Halflooper got in around 8:00 the following night. Of course, we had to stay on to attend the rally. The weekend included a poker run, a vendor display, demos on new and upcoming watercraft, a radar speed check, one heck of a cookout, and, to end it, a bikini contest. As usual, I lost the bikini contest! At one point during the weekend, Halflooper and I went out riding about an hour before the others. As we were coming back to the marina, all we could see in the distance was the spray from 160 Bumblebees coming straight at us at 50 miles per hour. What a sight!

The St. Augustine Bumblebee Rally

On September 16, we headed north from St. Augustine, the last leg of the journey. From then on, weather alerts would be critical. Going north on the ICW was not protected, unlike the previous stretch along Florida. North winds could create havoc there. I didn't want to get stopped by a hurricane with only days left to go in the trip.

We stopped at Fernandino Beach, right on the Florida/Georgia state line. The next day, September 17, we left for Savannah, Georgia. It was a wonderful run with flat land, grass, palm and pine trees, and sand beaches. There the ICW was as wide as 100 feet with large, open sounds three to four miles wide that opened out into the ocean. The ICW was well marked for the most part, but in the sounds the markers were hard to pick out from three feet above water. The GPS covered its cost many times over in those open sounds.

We stopped for lunch at the Half Moon Bay Marina. For Bumblebees it was a required stop for fuel. That afternoon we arrived at a marina outside Savannah and hailed a taxi for the city. Savannah was one of those special Southern cities with wonderful restaurants, quaint shops, and a rich history.

The next day we planned to make the run to Beaufort, South Carolina. But that morning when I came out to the marina, I couldn't see the Bumblebee. It had sunk, but the lines still held it to the dock. After removing the seat, I could see that the engine compartment was flooded. Not another dead Bumblebee! There was no way I could replace it in time to reach Virginia Beach before September 30. Just when I thought it was going to be easy, the trip had turned difficult again.

First things first. I got a manual bilge pump and removed most of the water. Then Halflooper towed me to the marina services, where they hoisted the Bumblebee out of the water. Within 30 minutes the marina crew had the Bumblebee on its way to the dealer. The mechanic went to work and discovered that the main shaft in the rear of the Bumblebee had a hard rubber silicone washer that had worn out. It didn't leak when I was traveling, but when I stopped, it took on water. The dealer couldn't get the part for two days, and that put us in Savannah for two unplanned days. Of course it was a great city to be stuck in, but I was getting more and more anxious about reaching Virginia Beach by September 30.

From: waverider4222@palm.com

Sent: Wednesday, September 18, 2002 3:54 PM

To: all@all.com

Subject: Where's LArRy NOW''

Well I spent the weekend in St Augustine at a PowerWaterCraft show, which attracted 160 jet skiers. Not sure if I mentioned or not but I have little business cards that I give out that tells about the adventure that I am taking: well I put a card in 5 bottles and released them in the ocean; so if anyone gets them please let me know,,, only one thing happen odd at the Conch

House Motel, I woke up one morning and the bed was soaked,,,no I did not have an accident,,,but the bed was totaly wet,,,with water ,,,hummmmm,,,well sure enough,,on the ceiling over the bed was the a/c exhaust and it had released condensation all night,,,so just another item to look for in motel world,,headed north from St Augustine has been wonderful (passed the 5,000 mile mark),, the intercoastal waterway is fantastic and words can not put it into perspective and I know the pictures will not do it justice. You have big "Sounds " coming in from the Atlantic Ocean and waterways that traverse east to west and west to east,,with lots of porpise that are extremely friendly,,stop at one point and 2 came up within 2 feet of the jet ski ,,,real neat,,I have traveled this area so it has some great places to stop,,,,on the last leg of the trip and you will only get one final email,,yes I know all will be sad,,,but everything must come to an END. Lastly, I am a great planner and try anticipate issues; well I would not have expected to leave the jet ski overnoght at the marina only to return and jet ski sunk at the dock , creates an interesting day, this is begining to test my wits!

NO I DONOT GET A MONEY IF YOU LOOK AT THE WEB SITE

Larry

On top of the jet ski breakdown, two hurricanes were gathering strength and could have been coming our direction. One hurricane was in the lower Caribbean, and another was in the Gulf of Mexico. I had already dodged three hurricanes. Each time I had been south of the storm. But that wasn't so certain. I was getting very nervous.

On September 20, the jet ski was ready to roll at about 3 p.m. We made the short run to Beaufort. It was really a test run for the jet ski. I had to be sure it was fixed, and I didn't want to be so far I couldn't get back to the dealer if there were problems. Beaufort was a great little city with a quaint downtown, and, by all means, you should stop and have cocktails and dinner at Emily's, an East Coast keeper. The unexpected delay in Savanna had put us behind. My total miles on the Loop were 5,223, with 577 miles remaining.

Charleston, South Carolina, was the destination on September 21. It was an uneventful run with smooth waters. We both wanted to spend more time in that great city, but the hurricanes were heading our way. I still had 488 miles to run.

The next morning, September 22, I knew time was running out. One hurricane had come onshore around New Orleans and was headed northeast. Another hurricane was in the Atlantic headed west toward North Carolina. I knew it was going to be a run for the money. We got out early, and the run from Charleston to Myrtle Beach was one of the best of the trip. It was peaceful and flat, and the water was like glass. Wind was not a problem. We stopped in North Myrtle Beach, 121 miles for the day.

I was watching both hurricanes and constantly checking the weather. I reviewed it with Halflooper. We were going to be facing bad weather fast. But Halflooper never bothered himself about such things. We had 367 miles left, and that, to him, seemed like a walk in the park. I wasn't so sure. With the help of the Weather Channel and charts, I explained to Halflooper that we had two choices. We could stay there until the two hurricanes had blown over, which would have us on land for seven days. That day was September 21. That was cutting it awfully close. We could make the 367 miles in two days, but those hurricanes were still out there, and we could get caught. The idea that Jim might still win the bet eliminated that choice with very little discussion. Even if Halflooper had wanted to stay, I would have used my captain's vote to push ahead.

The next day, we had to make 168 miles. We were shooting for a small city called Oriental, North Carolina. That was the first day of fall, and we started out with fog over the water. But it turned into a great day, and we had an excellent 100 miles. Then the rain started. When I heard the lightning, I headed for land. We stopped in Wrightsville Beach and had breakfast and waited it out for about two hours.

Then we set off again. The final run to Oriental was a test of will or stupidity. We came out of the ICW and then across the Neuse River to Oriental, which was on the other side. It was about five miles across. We were trailing a 65-foot Hatteras. It was running wide open, moving at about 25 knots. The storm was moving right up the water from east to west. We were going right into it. When that Hatteras (which I knew had the latest electronic gear) did a U-turn and came back at us at 25 knots, I knew it was one hell of a storm in front of us. The clouds were rolling up above us, black and foreboding, with every indication that we could get waterspouts and lightning.

When we hit the river, I yelled to Halflooper, "Every man for himself! See you in Oriental!" We both opened up the throttles. It was the fastest five miles either one of us ever did. I was saying my prayers. For a minute or so, I thought I had lost Halflooper, and then out of the dark he appeared, and I didn't have to make a missing persons report.

That evening, Halflooper was uncharacteristically interested in the weather report. Despite continuing bad weather predictions, we voted to go ahead. Otherwise it was highly likely I wouldn't get in by September 30. I thought the size of the mosquitoes in Oriental convinced Halflooper not to spend seven days there.

September 24. Only 199 miles left. The wind was coming out of the northeast, with waves from four to eight feet high. That was going to be a serious challenge. We left Oriental and headed up the Neuse River. That was where we hit the worst of it, but luckily it was early in the morning, when we were at our strongest. For 25 miles we fought the waves of six to eight feet and moved about five miles per hour. It was Lake Erie's equal. At one point, Halflooper looked down in the well of his jet ski, and he had a small fish riding with him. We took a break to refuel and recover our strength and set free small marine life. We reached the ICW channel, and the water smoothed out for about 20 miles. We needed that respite. After that, it was out into Alligator River. Again, the waves were hitting at three to five feet high. The next 25 miles were hard and tiring; we made between only five and 10 miles per hour. Exhaustion was setting in. We could drink only so much water and fight only so many waves.

We came into the southwest side of Albemarle Sound to refuel and try to recover. We were both beat. Ms. Wanda's restaurant was a safe haven but not a place to stay. We still had 30 miles to go, and it would be across the Albemarle Sound. Halflooper called for a vote. Continue or stop? I suggested we have our fried chicken first and then vote. (I knew I had a better chance of convincing him to go on if he had a full stomach.) Over the meal, we discussed the pros and cons of continuing. We discussed both sides thoroughly. Even with a full stomach, Halflooper wanted to stop and search out a motel. I wanted to keep going and get across Albemarle Sound. The hurricanes were still coming north. Albemarle Sound would be impossible to cross in 24 hours. I voted go. Halflooper said no. It was a Mexican standoff. I couldn't budge him. He'd had enough. I decided to call his bluff. I got on my Bumblebee and started the engine, ready to leave. I knew I would never leave him, but I also knew he'd jump on his Bumblebee and follow me. He wouldn't be happy about it, but he was one tough guy.

Sure enough, Halflooper did as I predicted, and we both took off across the Albemarle Sound. The waves were as bad as we thought they would be—three to four feet high. It was hard riding. In fact, it was one of the hardest days of the entire trip around the Loop. But we made it to our objective, Coinjock, North Carolina. It was a 149-mile test of endurance. When we finished, Halflooper and I knew we had achieved something, even if no one would ever know but us two.

I did not know what to expect the next day, the last day of the trip. I couldn't believe it would be as hard as the previous day. That evening

I asked myself whether the whole trip had been worth it. Yes. Would I do it again? Yes. Would I miss traveling the waterways? Yes. The trip had been a test of physical endurance, but there were so many other benefits of the trip that I couldn't put into words. There were all the wonderful places and people, the beauty of the waterways that no words could ever capture. I wished I could put it into words so that others could see it through my eyes. I called my wife and mother that night and told them we'd be coming into the 64th Street pier the next afternoon.

Dawn broke on September 25, the last day of my trip around the Great American Loop. The last run! It would cover 81 miles. Because I was born and raised in the area, I knew what to expect. The weather prediction said the northeast winds would be blowing at 15 to 25 miles per hour, but we were still north of the hurricanes. Halflooper looked dubious when he asked about the weather for the day. "Cupcake weather conditions," I said. (Hmmm, was I lying?)

I expected the run to be about four hours, but it could turn tough if we had to go out into the Chesapeake Bay and fight strong waves. From Coinjock to the Currituck Sound was about 12 miles. The waves were hitting from one to three feet high. Once we crossed the sound, we were in Virginia. In Virginia, the waterways slimmed out, making the run nice and smooth.

We stopped just south of the Chesapeake lock. We fueled up for the last time and waited for the lock to open. Then we got in the front of the line going into the lock. The lockmaster called on the VHF and asked that we go in alone. That was odd. Halflooper and I glanced at each other, puzzled. Why would the lockmaster want us to go in alone? "Why?" I asked over the VHF.

The lockmaster explained that there was a manatee in the lock. He wanted us to help flush the manatee out. Wow! If any craft could do that job without hurting the manatee, the lockmaster figured it was a Bumblebee. The Bumblebee had no props to scar or maim the sea cow. The lockmaster opened the lock, and in we went. At first, we didn't see the manatee. After going back and forth for about an hour, the lockmaster concluded that the manatee must have escaped through the open end of the lock. The lockmaster opened the gate up for more boats to enter. A barge and a tug heading north entered the lock with us. As we sat waiting for the water level to rise in the lock, the manatee raised its whiskered head and looked at us. It was a big one, at least 1,000 pounds. It was just feet away from me. It looked right at me, as though it had popped right out of one of my dreams. I smiled in response, and I'd swear the manatee smiled back.

The lockmaster opened the gate. We moved out, but the lockmaster wouldn't allow the tug operator to start his engines because the deep props could hurt the sea cow. The manatee ruled the lock. We left him in charge.

On the northern side, at least 25 yachts were waiting to go through the lock. I couldn't believe I'd had this gift on the last day of the run. A manatee right there with me!

Our route took us into Norfolk, which has the largest East Coast naval base. I felt very tiny on the jet ski when going past those 1,000-foot-plus aircraft carriers. Then it was out into the Elizabeth River and into the Chesapeake Bay. By that time, the ride was getting rough, and waves were hitting at four to six feet high. We turned south toward Virginia Beach, with about 20 miles left. Even with the winds at our back, the heavy waves took a toll on us. Then I saw the Chesapeake Bay Bridge, which spanned the mouth of the Chesapeake Bay and separated it from the Atlantic Ocean. That meant we had about three miles remaining before we hit the calm waters of Lynnhaven Inlet.

I would never forget the moment when we both went under the Lynnhaven Bridge. Our arms flew up in the air in triumph. Yes! We had made it. I had finished the Great American Loop! I had traveled 5,800 miles through all kinds of waters and landscapes and conditions.

The Bumblebee makes it home to Virginia Beach, Virginia

I told Halflooper to open up the throttle for the last run into 64th Street. I knew my family was waiting at the dock. I headed for port at 60 miles per hour. Then a honeybee hit my hand with such force that a stinger went right into my finger. What were the odds? Go figure. Mother Nature got in one last punch. But that didn't slow me down. About 300 feet offshore, I did a 360 donut on the jet ski at full throttle.

On dock, I was greeted by my wife and mother and other well-wishers. Several who had just won money from Jim were cheering wildly. My mother, not known for that sort of gesture, presented me with a plaque of accomplishment that read "American Great Loop 5,800 miles Larry G. Harcum September 25." I had been and seen many places, but that plaque meant more to me than all the tea in China. I was proud as a peacock!

Proud as a peacock

Mom and me

Epilogue

Was this a record? First, let me say that I didn't start with the idea of setting a record. John Moffett completed the Loop in 81 days, traveling 5,601 miles and using two jet skis. My goal was to complete the Great American Loop but, as much as possible, at my own pace. I wanted to see the cities and the beauty of the land.

I will give you the statistics, and you make your own decision. I left Virginia Beach, Virginia, on May 24. I arrived back at the same port 115 days later. Out of those 115 days, I was laid up healing for 28 days, which put me on the water traveling for 87 days. The 28-day healing delay was definitely not planned, but I am grateful that I still had the time to get back in the water and complete the Loop before it got too cold for such a journey. But, no, I did not achieve the time record for the Great American Loop. John Moffett, as far as I know, still holds that distinction.

Without the accident, could I have beaten the time record? Yes, but I do not think I wanted to beat the time record. I wanted to see America.

What about the miles record? John Moffett completed 5,601 continuous miles with no interruption. Again, I did not set out to beat the distance record. I did not originally think of going around Key West. That thought came to me when I was in Chicago and realized I had a connection in Fort Myers Beach who was willing to hire a leader boat to assist me with fuel so that I could circle Key West and make the distance record. So, in total, I rode 5,805.5 miles in 87 days, but those were not continuous days.

Is this a record? You make the decision. For me, it was a record, and that's what counts. I did it, and no one can take that away from me. I visited 19 states and one other country (Canada). I stayed at 80-plus motels and hotels and traveled on the Bumblebee 284.5 hours with two four-stroke jet skis.

Nick's marquee welcomed me home and celebrated my journey

Can the Loop be done in fewer than 81 days? Yes.

But that is not the real question. Do you want to do it? If you do, don't waste the adventure trying to make a record. Enjoy the adventure itself. Enjoy what you have never seen. Experience what you may never experience again. The record is not the point. The adventure is the point. I hope to see you out there!

These days I often get the question, "What are you going to do now to top this?" Challenges are constant. I set my own records. But I know I cannot sit still too long. Soon a dream begins to form and then a plan, and then the plan becomes a reality. Keep your dreams. Make them happen. Do not wait until it's too late. Do not say, "I wish I had done that." Go wherever your dreams take you! Remember: "Every day is Saturday!"